The Times

Letters from South Africa

The Times

Letters from South Africa

ISBN/EAN: 9783744757553

Printed in Europe, USA, Canada, Australia, Japan

Cover: Foto ©ninafisch / pixelio.de

More available books at **www.hansebooks.com**

BY

𝕿𝖍𝖊 𝕿𝖎𝖒𝖊𝖘 SPECIAL CORRESPONDENT

Reprinted from 𝕿𝖍𝖊 𝕿𝖎𝖒𝖊𝖘
of July, August, September, and October 1892

𝕷𝖔𝖓𝖉𝖔𝖓

MACMILLAN AND CO.

AND NEW YORK

AND 𝕿𝖍𝖊 𝕿𝖎𝖒𝖊𝖘 OFFICE, PRINTING HOUSE SQUARE

1893

All rights reserved

THESE Letters are reprinted as they originally appeared in the columns of *The Times*, at the request of several of the most prominent public men in South Africa, who, though representing various shades of political opinion, unite in saying that the situation as it exists at present is faithfully reflected in these pages, and in expressing a wish that the general public should by their republication have the opportunity of becoming better acquainted with South African affairs.

THE TIMES OFFICE, PRINTING HOUSE SQUARE,
LONDON, *January* 1893.

I

KIMBERLEY.

UP to the Karoo! It means up from Cape Town, which is on the level of the sea, to a plateau topping the summit of Table Mountain, and maintaining throughout the extent of half a continent an elevation of from 3000 to 6000 feet. The principal climb is done in the first twelve hours of a railway journey. A train leaves Cape Town at nine in the evening. Through the night the traveller, struggling with a first experience of railway beds, which he afterwards learns to regard as quite sufficiently comfortable for sleeping purposes, hears the almost human groan and strain of the engine as it toils up the heavy way. There is even a point at which his dreams fill themselves with a futile sense of pushing. The slow pace, the many stoppages, the sound of voices into the cause of which he is scarcely awake enough to inquire, combine to convey the impression that every official and servant of the road is lending muscle to assist the locomotive. An attempt to remove the baize with which the window is blinded for the night reveals nothing but outer darkness. In the morning he learns that he was in fact pushed by a second engine up the ascent of the Hex River Pass, where the gradient is 1 in 40 for 5 miles, and he wakes to find himself upon the Karoo.

The effect is magical. The world of trees and towns has been left behind; he is up in the country of the mountain-tops. On all sides they stretch away, peak behind peak, and range behind range, in every variety of shape and colour, from the clear browns and purples of the near foreground to the liquid blues and melting heliotrope and primrose of the horizon. There is no sign of habitation, and scarcely, at first, of animal life. The ground is covered with a gray-green scrub, of which the monotony is broken only here and there by a clump of mimosa bushes wearing their long white thorns like flowers, or by the sheer barrenness of patches of red shingle.

But at this season of the year it is probable that there has been a good deal of rain. The water is standing in pools and natural depressions, and the hues of the sunrise reflected in it give a colour to the whole scene which is indescribable. The air is keen, but so extraordinarily invigorating that you gladly throw down the windows of the carriage and let it play upon you without fear of cold. A sense of lightness which calls back childish dreams of flight possesses the body. The idea of reaching the distant ranges by a direct progress from peak to peak has not the patent impossibility that it would wear in Piccadilly.

Meantime the sunlight spreads, and the exhilaration produced by the fresh air finds more material expression in a well-developed appetite for breakfast. The train stops while this is gratified at Matjes-Fontein, a little invalid settlement, where about a dozen houses cluster round the station and hotel. Here a health station has been established where patients come to undergo the simple process of an air cure. Throughout the Karoo the stopping-places are all health stations, for while the soil in this part of the great plateau has not yet been put to any practical use, the air has been found to possess such remarkable curative power for diseases of the chest that people flock to it in increasing numbers year by year.

The Karoo proper is bounded on the north by the Roggeweld and Nieuweld mountains, and on the south by the Great and Little Zwartzenbergen, which run in almost straight lines east and west for a couple of hundred miles. The course of the railway lies from south-east to north-west, having these ranges always in differing aspects on the horizon, the offshoots from them advancing sometimes in outlying koppjes to the very rails, sometimes receding to the ranks of the parent hills, and leaving the desert to widen into monotonous sweeps of plain. Overhead the sky has an intense clear blue, not unbroken, but flecked like an English sky in some of its best April days with dazzling white clouds. There is nothing English to which the scene can be compared. The nearest parallel is to be gained by travelling on foot through the mountain-tops of Wales. Then magnify the distances in the same proportion as the pace of a train multiplies the rate of pedestrian progress, and you get some conception of the breadth and space. The immense size of the African continent is for the first time presented visibly to the mind. Through it all the train rushes on, with the telegraph wire as a symbol of still greater swiftness by its side, and from the window of the train there is occasional opportunity to note the very different progress of another form of travelling.

From time to time we pass the white tented cover of a wagon, in which it is probable that the principal domestic provisions of some Dutch householder are stored. The wagon is about 20 feet long, brilliantly painted in red and green and yellow. Its canvas roof shines like snow in the sun, and perhaps as many as sixteen or eighteen oxen are yoked by pairs in the team which draws it at a foot's pace across the desert. The driver walks by the side of his wheelers, the children of the family usually lag a little behind; and somewhere, not far, either in front or behind, a herd of cattle are alternately moving and grazing.

Oxen succeed in getting a living for themselves from the inhospitable-looking scrub, and for this, among other reasons, they are the preferred animals for wagon-travelling. For this reason, also, when a farmer moves he has no need to sell his cattle, but prefers to take them with him. You speed past. The slowly-moving party is hardly seen before it has been left far behind, and there may be hours again of solitude before any further sign of human existence meets the eye. Occasionally it happens that you pass a wretched hut set down in the centre of the waste. The train may even be obliged to slacken its pace in order to give time to clear the line of a flock of goats, which tells you that the desert has a native inhabitant who succeeds in drawing some poor sustenance from the soil. But he scarcely interests you.

The sense of travel in its positive sense, so different from the mere negative withdrawal from London, has filled you. Increasingly as the hours pass by and the clear noonday light begins to deepen into sunset, you realise that you are going into new country, and your feeling of fellowship is stirred for the man with the wagon, who, like yourself, has felt the attraction that lies on the other side of the Karoo. You, in your progressive English fashion, must hurry as fast as steam and electricity can take you. He, in his traditional Dutch manner, is content to move on slowly day by day. He calls his progress "trekking." You give the name of travelling to yours. Each is alike removed from the stationary condition of the goat-herd in the hut. Each has a distinct aim towards which he is tending, and each, it strikes you, is for the moment representative of a force at work upon South Africa. The Dutchman is going to seek one form of natural wealth. In his ultimate place of settlement he desires to find pasturage for his cattle and seed earth for his corn. Space is essential to him, and space alone. He has no need to hurry, no need to keep pace with modern inventions. Time is on his side, and the patient process of the seasons will bring his fortune almost without labour from the soil.

The destination of the Englishman in his typical character is one of the mining centres. He is going to Kimberley or Johannesburg, or it may be to the still unproved gold-fields of Mashonaland. He wants profit, but he wants it quickly. He has no time to seek it in leisurely fashion, behind slow-plodding oxen, surrounded by his baby children and his women. When the Dutch trekker is preparing to "outspan" for the evening meal, the day's journey finished only a few miles beyond the spot at which he was seen at noon, the train has already reached Beaufort West at the north-eastern extremity of this section of the Karoo. A crowd of consumptive invalids has come there, as at other places, to greet the friends or the friends of friends who are passing through, and before night closes we are hurrying on over the Winterveldt to Kimberley.

In the morning the character of the landscape has changed. We have crossed the Orange River, the mountains have drawn back to the distant horizon, and the plain, covered by rough scrubby grass, has widened on every side. The air is frosty, and we are glad of all our wraps, but by nine o'clock, when we reach Kimberley Station, the sun is already warm enough to produce the illusion of a summer day. It is really mid-winter; chrysanthemums have all been cut down by the frost. Only the hardier sorts of roses, geraniums, violets, and autumn foliage linger still in the villa gardens, which are springing up in English fashion round the town. It has taken thirty-six hours to do 547 miles, including the ascent from Cape Town, but the railway arrangements are comfortable enough to render the journey possible without too great fatigue, and the day lies before any one who chooses to see the diamond mines.

It is so impossible to speak of Kimberley without speaking of the diamond mines that, at the risk of repeating what has been told a thousand times before, I describe them as they were shown to me, with all their dependencies of labour settlements. They concentrate round them almost the entire life of Kimberley, and they illustrate some of the most interesting questions which are connected with the development of enterprise in South Africa. The most logical way of seeing the process of extraction is to begin underground and brave at once the slush and heat and drip of the 800 feet level. Here, while you splash, candle in hand, in the darkness, through some two or three miles of labyrinthine passages, you have time to realise the work which is being done by the thousands of natives who are busy day and night throughout a honeycombed depth of 1100 feet in getting out the blue earth from its bed. There is no reef. The whole mass of the mine is diamondiferous, the rich stuff descends apparently to limitless depths, and all that has to be done is to bring it to the surface in such a manner that gallery shall still stand on gallery and allow of working without danger of collapse. Above, below, on every side you hear the sound of pick-and-rock drill and rolling trucks. Black figures glue themselves against the walls to let you pass.

The conditions of the scene combine to produce a vivid impression of labour. The natives work together in gangs of four, filling the trucks. Perspiration pearls over their naked bodies in some of the hottest galleries, but they appear to labour without distress. In the main galleries, which are admirably ventilated, they are for the most part fully dressed. They work either by time or task as they please, their wages remaining the same in either case; and I was told that they often finish their allotted number of trucks in two-thirds of the time which is allowed. Seeing what they do and how easily they do it, you can never doubt any more that the African native is able to work, and to work well when he chooses. The pleasanter processes of diamond-mining begin when you follow the contents of the trucks up to welcome daylight again, and see the "blue," as it is familiarly called, laid out on the floors. The "floors" are simply fields fenced round with high wire fences, where the extracted rock is spread out in beds of a certain thickness to pulverise under the action of the air. The contents of the trucks as they are emptied out run themselves into long rows; the colour of the stuff is almost identical with the gray-purplish hue of winter cabbages at home, and at first sight the flat and widespreading floors might easily be mistaken for Essex cabbage fields.

The process of pulverisation takes from four to six months, according to the weather and the condition of the rock, and it is assisted by operations of watering and rolling, which add to the agricultural illusion. The average yield of every load of blue is one carat of diamonds, and as the average net profit on a carat of diamonds is about 20s., the value of the million loads, which I was told that I was looking at in the extent of a couple of cabbage fields, is not far from £1,000,000 sterling. As soon as the blue is sufficiently pulverised it is taken to the washing machine, where, by means of an ingenious system of water flowing over revolving pans, the lighter part of the earth is washed away, while the heavier remains in the bottom of the pans. By this process 99 per cent of the blue earth is got rid of, and of 100 loads which go into the washing machine only one is saved to be sorted. The remaining 99, after passing through the various sieves and stages of the washing machine, pour out in a state of liquid mud at the bottom of the machine, and are carted away by mechanical haulage to be emptied on the daily increasing hillocks of diamond tailings, which, if other records of the industry were to vanish, might well puzzle future geologists to account for their composition. The weight of diamonds keeps the precious stones for the most part with the heavy residue which has been saved.

It is, however, well known that a considerable quantity of diamondiferous stuff escapes with the tailings, and if any economical process of treating them could be discovered, the mounds of apparently water-worn rock which dot the neighbourhood would suddenly acquire a new value. So far no practical use for this waste earth has been discovered. The one rich load to which the hundred raw loads have been reduced in passing through the washing machine was at one time sorted by hand. It is now subjected to a further preliminary of washing and sorting in a machine known as the pulsator. Here the diamondiferous stuff is passed under water over pulsating screens, in which a double layer of leaden bullets has been placed. The pulsating motion causes a constant gentle shaking to be maintained, and as the specific gravity of diamonds is greater than that of lead, while the specific gravity of much of the waste pebbly material is less, the effect is to shake the diamonds to the bottom of the shot, while the waste material remains above it, and is gradually washed over the side of the screen by the running water. The diamondiferous stuff is served into these wet pans by means of a cylindrical sieve, which distributes the finest from one end and the coarsest from the other, with regulated gradations between, on the same principle as the main sieve of an ordinary flour mill.

The whole process of mechanical sorting is based upon the relative weight of the diamond to other stones of the same size among which it is found, and if the difference were as great as the difference between the weight of gold and the mineral substances from which it is divided by washing there would be little waste and much less hand labour. As it is, many stones, such as garnets and others of no value, of which the specific gravity is equal to that of diamonds, are found in the diamondiferous earth. These, of course, pass in the pulsator through the bed, and when all has been done that can be done by mechanical processes, the material which is taken from the machine has still to be subjected to the slow, uncertain, and costly process of hand sorting, with all its temptations to dishonesty.

In the sorting room the first thing which strikes you with surprise is to perceive that native convicts are busy at the sorting tables. Almost all the sentences at the convict station are inflicted for theft, and the handling of uncounted diamonds seems the last work upon which it would be desirable to employ convicted thieves. However, as a matter of fact, it is found that the greater hold which it is possible to have over a convict, and the greater difficulty which they experience in being able either to keep or to dispose of stolen diamonds in prison, makes them really safer to employ than the average free coloured labourer. They are trusted only with the smaller-grained stuff, in which the smaller diamonds are found.

More than this, after you have stood for some time by one of the tables, where four men are employed, you probably become aware of an indefinite sensation of discomfort, and raising your head you perceive that a white man, whose business it is to watch the proceedings of every one below, is seated upon a beam overhead. No one employed can be sure at any moment that the eye of a watcher is not upon him. The larger-grained stuff is all sorted by trusted white men. The mass of pebbles which the distribution of the cylindrical sieve has already sorted according to size are carried into this room in hand sieves and thrown in wet heaps upon their respective tables, where every sorter is provided with a flat metal slice and a little covered tin pannikin into which each diamond as it is found is dropped. With the metal slice a small portion of the mass is scattered rapidly over the table, inspected, and swept over the side.

The rapidity with which a practised sorter is able to detect a diamond or decide upon the absence of any in the portion scattered is astonishing to the amateur beholder, who can hardly believe that there has been time to look before the refuse has been swept off the board. Doubtless valuable stones are sometimes missed and a percentage of loss must be reckoned with. In order to guard against it, especially in the larger-grained stuff, the whole refuse of the sorting is carried out and spread upon sacks in the yard, where men are employed to sort it a second time. The quantity of recovered diamonds is sufficient to justify the precaution, but it is not very great. The diamonds from the sorting room are made into parcels twice a day, and sent under armed escort to the office, where they are again sorted for commercial purposes by practised valuers. It is in this office that the great variety as well as beauty of the stones can be appreciated. There are specimens cut and uncut of every kind and colour. After the white diamond the yellow is the most frequent, but there are also stones of green and purple, pink, blue, and almost black shades, in which brilliancy and colour appear to combine for their very highest expression. Here the industry is lost sight of, and the gem value of the diamonds asserts itself.

II

KIMBERLEY.

PERHAPS the most interesting part of the Kimberley mines is the manner in which the De Beers Company have dealt with the difficult labour question of the country. The mines employ three kinds of labour —convicts, free natives, and white men. The convicts may be left out of count as constituting only a small and abnormal element, and the numbers which remain are 6000 natives and 1400 whites, exclusive of superior officials. The average wages are £1 a week for the natives, and from £3 : 10s. a week upwards for the white man. Mr. Rhodes was heard to say in a London drawing-room last year that it was the reading of *Germinal* which had caused him to realise the necessity of providing decent homes and harmless pleasures for the Kimberley miners. If so, the fact marks Kimberley as a curious link between the double chains of European and African experience which meet here abruptly, and M. Zola can have the pleasure of knowing that there is at least one work of his which has not been barren of fruit. All the men employed in the De Beers mine have homes provided for them suitable to their condition.

The village of Kenilworth, where the white men

live, is Mr. Rhodes's special personal hobby. It is on the De Beers estate, at a distance of about a mile and a half from the town and mine. A tram takes the men to and from their work. The first charm of the place, situated in a naturally treeless plain, near a town of corrugated iron, is that it has been well planted with eucalyptus trees and shrubs and vines, and that the houses are of pleasing architectural designs, built chiefly of brick and wood. They stand either singly or in pairs in their own gardens. The centre of the settlement is a clubhouse, which is surrounded by its own well-kept grounds, and includes library, billiard-rooms, reading-rooms, and dining-hall. The houses in which quarters are let to single men stand nearest to it, and the dining-hall is habitually used as a common mess. The feeding arrangements are made by contract with a caterer, to whom each man pays 25s. a week.

Dinner for the evening shift was in course of preparation as we passed through the kitchen, and consisted of soup, two *entrées*, and five or six joints, with vegetables and sweets. The tables in the large, cool dining-room were laid with clean cloths and table napkins, and the whole tone and aspect of the establishment were of a kind in which a cultivated man could live without loss of decency or self-respect. People were sauntering in and out of the reading-room with illustrated papers in their hands to enjoy the last sunshine on the verandah. The garden was a mass of flowers. A young couple were walking away under a long vine trellis known as the Lovers' Walk.

At nightfall, when the sun is gone, the air becomes

again sharply cold. Then fires would be lit, I was told, in the principal rooms, and the place would fill for the evening. With the recollection of some of our own mining towns in my mind and a remembrance of the picture presented by the book from which this settlement had sprung, it seemed scarcely credible to me that this could be the everyday aspect of a miner's home life in Africa. Yet every question I asked drew only answers which assured me that, with a due allowance for the inevitable irregularities of human nature, it represented, not only the superficial appearance, but the everyday habits which correspond to an appearance of respectability, comfort, and intelligence. Single men in this settlement pay £1 a month for their quarters. This, with the 25s. a week for their board, leaves them still a handsome margin of wages. The most expensive married quarters, which look like pretty little villas outside, and are fitted with every convenience within, cost £5 a month. I asked how the scheme answered from the financial point of view, and was told that it yields an interest of 5 per cent upon the invested capital. The present settlement is only large enough to accommodate the workmen of the De Beers mine. It is, however, in contemplation to make an extension which shall take in the workmen of the Kimberley mine also.

From this practical recognition of the principle of equality between man and man, it was at once striking and interesting to drive to one of the "compounds" or locations which are provided for the native labourers. In order to check drunkenness and diamond-stealing among the natives it has been found absolutely necessary to place them under supervision during the term of their engagement in the mine. Every native labourer who is employed by the De Beers Company engages to live in one of the company's compounds and to obey its regulations, and from the day he enters the compound he does not again leave it until he is discharged or has obtained a formal leave of absence. He sees his wives and family, if they choose to visit him, in the presence of an overseer, and he speaks to them through a grating. He never approaches so close to them as to be able under any pretence to pass a diamond from one hand to another.

The compound communicates by means of a covered way with the mine to which he goes for his work. Except to work he has no communication with the world. The conditions of seclusion are as absolute as those of the life of any monk, and the compound is described in one sentence when it is called a monastery of labour. Yet the compounds are voluntarily filled to the required number, and many of their inhabitants have, with occasional leave of absence, remained in them for years. The one which we visited contained when it was full about 2600 men. Nine hundred were absent in the mine. The remaining 1700 were busy with the preparation of their evening meal. The sun was setting over the roofs of the huts, which enclose a great square.

A few dusky figures, wrapped in blankets mostly of a bright terra-cotta colour, caught the eye as they moved in the light of the last rays, but twilight shadows had already fallen upon the greater part of the courtyard. Perhaps as many as a hundred fires blazed before the open doors of the huts, and round each fire a circle was gathered of natives, dressed and undressed, varying in degrees of duskiness, but all alike composing groups in the warm flame-light, with now a face here, an arm or a leg there, thrown into sharp relief that would have defied either painter or sculptor to reproduce. From black and gray and smoke-colour to the high lights of burnished copper, rendered sharper by the white and blue tongues of the blazing wood, no gradation was missing. Large three-legged pots were pushed into the embers and presided over by one or two members of each circle. The remainder, while they waited for their supper, were engaged in chatting, smoking, and playing a game with pebbles upon a sort of chess-board marked out in the earth, which is, I was told, almost as classic an amusement among African natives as chess among their Aryan cousins. Upon investigation we found that the contents of the supper-pots varied a good deal, each man or group providing as they pleased for their own wants.

Wages are high, and every form of food material which is likely to be required can be obtained at reasonable prices in the canteen of the compound. Intoxicating liquor is, of course, absolutely excluded, but tea, coffee, and a variety of harmless drinks are to be bought, and the crowd which filled the canteen when we visited it testified to the fact that the pleasures or necessities of the commissariat are by no means neglected. Wood and water are furnished without cost. Natives from all parts of South Africa live together harmoniously in one compound, but the custom is for the various tribes to have their separate huts and messing arrangements. Marked differences were observable in the

C

facial and other characteristics of the several groups, and the working capacity of the different tribes is found to vary in no less marked a degree. The common opinion here and elsewhere appeared to be that the Zulu and Basuto natives far surpass all others in industry and adaptability to the requirements of civilised labour. The comforts of the compound include swimming baths and a hospital, where, in the accident ward, a number of natives were amusing themselves with part-singing and looked extremely cheerful. The only part of the whole establishment in which the note of buoyant good spirits appeared to flag was in the fever ward. Here alone black heads lay languid on the pillows, and the flash of white teeth in a ready laugh did not greet our entrance.

Scarcely any difficulty, the manager assured us, is experienced in the peaceful administration of the compound. Each compound is, of course, under white supervision. The men are usually satisfied with the arrangements made for their comfort; quarrelling between them is rare, thieving from one another is scarcely known, and when subjects of dispute arise they are disposed of by appeal to the white chief. The percentage of sickness is also low. As a means of obtaining the *maximum* amount of regular labour with a *minimum* of diamond-stealing, drunkenness, and annoyance to the surrounding population, the system has answered admirably, and that it is popular among the natives themselves seems to be scarcely doubtful. It is excessively interesting, because it shows that it is possible to get labour from the native, and to enable him to earn a fair wage without immediately spending it in drink. It explodes also the theory current among some employers of labour, that the native is ignorant of the value of money and cannot be attracted by high pay.

In the presence of the well-filled compounds there can be no question that the material advantages which they offer are as fully appreciated by the natives as are the advantages of Kenilworth by the white man. The two together may claim to have created conditions of life which satisfy both the white man and the native. The native is recognised as the motor power by means of which material development is carried out; the white man takes the position of director of this motor power, which is the only position that he can hold with satisfaction to himself in the African climate. Muscle on the one side and brain on the other must, for a long time to come, represent the respective contributions of the two races to the public stock.

The merit of the method by which the Kimberley mines are worked is that it acknowledges the fact without sacrificing either the black man to the white, or the white man to the black. So far, its value as an example can hardly be overrated. The objection is that in relation to the natives the system is not a natural one, and, however successful it may have proved itself under liberal management, the conditions are too evidently artificial to be suitable for universal application. It shows what is wanted, and it illustrates the result which may be obtained. Beyond this it cannot be said to carry a solution of the general problem which is perplexing South Africa. The farmer, the shopkeeper, the printer, the petty industrialist all over the country is unable to offer high wages as a bait, and to segregate his workmen in compounds from which external temptations cannot lure them. The schemes of compulsory labour which have from time to time been devised fall to the ground because the difficulty of finding one which is not slavery in disguise has hitherto proved insuperable, and without compulsion it has so far been found that the ordinary native is like his ordinary fellow-man in this—that he does not care to work after his most pressing wants have been satisfied. A wife is soon bought, a hut is soon built, and when these objects have been accomplished, he defies white energy by preferring a pipe in the sun to all the luxuries which continued labour could accumulate.

Like many another problem which seems at first sight insoluble, the labour problem may be expected to yield before the constant pressure of civilised effort, and the difficulties attaching to it which the De Beers Company have surmounted for themselves in their own energetic way have not prevented the conception of other enterprise, even in Kimberley itself. The town is full of sanguine expectation with regard to the result of the exhibition which is to open in September,[1] and the promoters of the undertaking very naturally hope that the effect of it will be productive of good throughout South Africa.

The preparation of the buildings and grounds is being very actively carried on, and is on a larger scale than any South African exhibition which has hitherto been attempted. The most practical interest will, of course, centre in the machinery court, into which, in order to facilitate the delivery of heavy goods, a branch line of rail has been run

[1] Written in June 1892.

from the Government railway. As the railway will be completed to Johannesburg and Pretoria before the exhibition closes, mining machinery which is exhibited at Kimberley and bought, as much of it probably will be, for use in the Transvaal, will thus have the advantage of arriving in the exhibition court and of being despatched to its final destination without having to bear the cost of one yard of wagon transport.

It is hoped and expected that the mining court will be unique in interest of its kind, for none has ever yet been shown so near to mining centres where the newest machinery is an urgent daily need, and the output which demonstrates the effect of it is so valuable. The De Beers Company will show such a collection of diamonds as has probably never come together before in any exhibition of the world as the produce of one mine, and Johannesburg will send the gold output of an entire month, representing a sum which, if the present rate of increase be maintained, will soon not fall far short of half a million sterling.

Special prizes have been awarded for diamond-mining and for gold-concentrating machinery, and in the presence of the diamonds and the gold even an uninstructed public may be expected to appreciate the interest attaching to the process of extraction. A dry concentrator for gold would make it possible to work many a mine which the absence of water now renders unpayable. In the Hopetown district alone there is an immense area covered with shale which contains gold-bearing copper ore. The ore runs 4 ounces to the ton; the quantity of it is practically unlimited, but the district is waterless, and machinery has yet to be found which will extract the ore without water from the shale. The value of a more perfect system of diamond-sorting will be realised by every visitor who spends a spare afternoon in the De Beers mine.

But mining interests are not the only ones which are to receive attention in the machinery court. Agricultural questions in a country of which the soil is so extraordinarily fertile present themselves in forms which are scarcely less novel, and are certainly not less important. For hundreds and hundreds of square miles in the neighbourhood of Kimberley the now bare veldt would, it is believed, bear crops of the same amazing richness as the cultivated portions of the Transvaal, if the waters of the Orange River, the Modder, and the Vaal could be saved from flowing, as they now flow, in mere waste out towards the sea. The average level of these river-beds is 60 feet below the average level of the land. Water-lifting machinery, which has done such wonders in Australia, would be no less valuable in application here, and Messrs. Chaffey Brothers have promised to put their Australian experience at the service of South Africa to the extent of sending experimental machinery purposely designed. Dairy machinery is also in much request, as well as other agricultural machinery suitable to farming on a large and varied scale.

Crops and methods in South Africa are undoubtedly more like those of Australia and America than of England, and it is perhaps natural that American and Australian machinery should appear to be beating our own out of the field. Nevertheless, from the English point of view it is infinitely regrettable to learn in face of such a manifestly opening market that English makers will no longer take the trouble to adapt their patterns to the new necessities created by the new conditions, and that alike in the departments of mining and agriculture they are losing ground every day. It is hardly, perhaps, realised at home how rapidly this transfer of trade is taking place, for the increase which, according to old doctrines of English manufacturing supremacy, ought to have come to England has only existed within the last few years. Four or five years ago English firms possessed the entire machinery trade of South Africa; but Johannesburg is only five years old, and at the present moment the American firm of Messrs. Fraser and Chalmers supplies at least 40 per cent of the mining machinery in use on the Rand.

American firms are active in sending representatives to study requirements on the spot, and every effort is made by them to adapt the new machines which they send out to the, in many cases, entirely new needs of the situation. It is a race between new patterns and excellence of material, in which latter quality English goods still hold their superiority, and new patterns are rapidly winning. The case of boilers is a typical one in point. Four years ago England had a monopoly of the boiler trade. Now, not only are American boilers in frequent use, but when a prize was offered at the exhibition for an improved form more suited to the fuel of the country, the principal American firm volunteered to send out a boiler, set it up, and work it at their own expense during the exhibition, while the best known English firms decline to compete, on the ground that their trade is fully established. So far is it, in truth, from being fully established, that it is in danger of disappearing altogether, and in all reasonable probability the result of the exhibition can only be to give a further push to its downward progress.

If the effect of the exhibition be in any degree to develop the gold-bearing and agricultural possibilities of the Kimberley district, and thus to redeem the town from its present position of depending exclusively upon the diamond industry, the primary object of the local organisation will be gained. In its wider scope of developing and adding to the knowledge already possessed of South African resources, and of the past history and future possibilities of this extraordinarily interesting portion of the continent, the opportunities offered by the exhibition are to be utilised for scientific and historic purposes. It is proposed especially to compile a practical handbook or manual of the mineral and agricultural resources of the country, for which purpose a committee has been named and circulars sent out inviting contributions in the form of both specimens and information from men of experience in all parts of the colonies and States.

Soil, water, climate, natural vegetation, crops, stock, mineral-bearing formations, systems of agriculture, fruit-growing, cattle-breeding, fisheries, and mining possibilities will all be made the subject of close and organised inquiry, and it is believed that a comparison of specimens and of the knowledge which many African visitors will bring in their own persons to the exhibition ought to result in the acquisition of a very valuable body of new facts. There will be native courts, which it is proposed to organise on the principle of the Japanese village at Kensington some years ago, showing the various native industries and natives at work upon them; and amongst the entertainments which are to take place in the central hall of the building there will be a series of lectures upon native history and habits.

The important question of the climate of South Africa in its relation to health is also to receive attention, and the Sanitary Congress will hold a sitting with this special object during the exhibition. The other conditions will be much like those of every exhibition which has been held of late years. All the space that was available for English and foreign courts has been engaged. There will be a ladies' court, showing the work and industries of the women of South Africa; and for that large majority of the public which does not look at the exhibits, there will be the usual entertainment in the way of music, illuminations, and refreshment rooms. There was a design to arrange the grounds as a botanic garden of South African plants. The difficulties in the way of carrying out the proposal have been found insurmountable in the available time, but as far as it is possible South African plants and flowers are to be brought together and shown in the fairly extensive gardens which surround the buildings. The contract for the nightly illumination has been taken by the same firm which is to light the World's Fair of Chicago, and an English band is to be imported for the occasion.

The really great obstacle to success which is presented by the distance of Kimberley from the coast has been, as far as possible, got over by the co-operation of the Cape Government in reducing the railway rates and furnishing special advantages in excursion trains, and correspondence with Messrs. Cook seems to promise the full complement of tourists which has been calculated as essential to a satisfactory balance of accounts. The idea is that the extension of the railway through the Transvaal, which will enable visitors to Kimberley to extend their trip, if they desire it, to Johannesburg, may, in combination with the charms of a South African spring, bring many holiday-makers, who will find the journey not much more expensive and the change and scope of travel much greater than that afforded by their usual autumn excursion. If this expectation prove correct, and South Africa be brought, as it well may be, under new developments of steamship and railway communication, into the ordinary beat of excursionist travel, the Kimberley Exhibition may fairly claim to have done a good deal for the material development of the country. One of the first requirements of South Africa in its present stage is to be seen. It teems with such astonishing possibilities that if that be achieved the rest may safely be left to time.

III

JOHANNESBURG.

THE journey from Kimberley to Vereeniging, on the Vaal River, which is at present the farthest extension of the railway, takes two days and two nights. When the cross-line from Kimberley to Bloemfontein is constructed through the Free State, and the necessity for going round three sides of a long parallelogram is got rid of, there will be a saving of about eighteen hours. Further improvements upon the northern part of the line may be expected to increase the speed, and the extension to Johannesburg, when all is finished, will bring that town within twenty-four hours of Kimberley. The connecting branch which is so much needed for the journey from Kimberley will not affect the railway distance from Cape Town, which has already been taken along the most direct line, and will measure something under a thousand miles to Johannesburg and Pretoria. Allowing for some moderate improvements in speed, it is hoped that before the end of the present year it may be possible to go direct from Cape Town to Johannesburg in two days and a half. The through trains will have sleeping-cars and kitchens attached to them, and the journey will entail comparatively little fatigue or discomfort.

The present terminus on the Transvaal side of the Vaal River is a mere engineer's camp upon the veldt. It has only been in existence for a few weeks, and is still a confusion of tents and railway sleepers, luggage and cooking pots, in the midst of which I noted, on the afternoon of our arrival, the characteristic detail of no fewer than six pianos waiting for the ox-wagons which were to carry them away. Passengers and their lighter luggage are still conveyed in the wonderful circus-like vehicles slung on leathern straps and drawn by a team of ten or twelve horses, which not long ago constituted the only means of communication. An experience of seven hours in one of them over a road deep in sand, intersected by streams and broken by unexpected outcroppings of rock, is enough to teach a hearty and grateful realisation of the comforts of the train. The team was changed five times, giving us in all sixty mules to do a journey of about 50 miles.

But coaches are already a thing of the past. In a very few months they will have ceased to exist upon this line of travel, and there is no need to dwell upon their miseries. At present the sense of connection broken with the outer world and the half-day's hard gallop over the bare veldt only heighten the effect of the town of Johannesburg when it is reached. It is neither beautiful nor impressive from the æsthetic point of view, but it might be set down as it stands in any part of the civilised world. It has a population of about 40,000. The buildings are good, the streets are broad; there are shops with plate-glass windows full of ball-dresses and silver plate; the residential quarters are rapidly spreading themselves out into squares and boulevards; a tram-line connects them with the business centre; for 20 miles east and west you may see the funnels of mining works smoking against the sky; the sound of an engine-whistle is in your ears, and you find that a train has been constructed which runs from one end of the Rand to the other. The town is lit with gas, water is supplied to all its houses, every ordinary appliance of civilisation is here; and, when you remember that it has all been done in five years, and that every scrap of material has been carried up, and the six pianos waiting at the frontier will presently be carried by ox-wagons, you begin to realise something of the extraordinary conditions which can have called so sudden a development into existence.

Johannesburg stands upon gold. When I wanted to have my conception of the position cleared, an engineer, who was showing me over one of the mines, took an enamelled iron basin and said: "Imagine this thing magnified in thickness, battered a little, and elongated to an irregular oval of which the longest axis is about 40 miles. If you like you can call the white enamel on the inside the hanging-wall, and the blue enamel on the outside the foot-wall. Thus the iron is the gold-bearing reef, and you have an imperfect model of what we believe we know of the gold formation of the Rand."

The object of all the mines which are situated upon the top edge of the lip is to get out the iron which represents the gold-bearing reef. The important question for each mine is the angle at which the reef descends through the ground which has been secured in surface claims; and the question of supreme importance for the future of the Witwatersrand gold industry as a whole is whether the gold reef does turn like the basin at the deep levels and lie along at a workable depth, or whether it goes away, still descending into the bowels of the earth. The model would have been more perfect if three basins had been put one inside another, for the conglomerate gold-bearing beds locally known as "Banket Reef" descend in three parallel lines. They have been proved in places where they dipped near the surface at an angle of 70 degrees to flatten at the 500 feet level to an angle of 30 degrees from the horizon. The immense advantage of this is evident, for a measurement of 3000 feet along the reef, which, if the lode were vertical might represent the limit of possible work, can here be reached at an actual depth of only 1500 feet from the surface. The flattening tendency of the angle of descent appears from the latest developments to continue. If it does, and if the reefs continue rich as they are near the surface, there will be no limit to the possible working until at some future time the entire gold reef has been removed.

Boring and sinking operations have proved that the reefs are, as a general rule, both larger and richer in the lower levels than in the upper levels; and, more than this, it has been found that, overlying the known series, there are in the lower levels other conglomerate beds of a workable size and value which give no indication whatever of their existence at or near the surface. In one place, at a depth of 600 feet, there are six lodes of payable size and value three of which show no sign on the surface, and only begin to appear in their broken lines of conglomerate pebbles at a depth of 300 feet. Indications of this kind open prospects of great speculative interest in the developments of the near future. There is an element of the unknown in it all, but it is of an unknown into which many incursions by way of experiment have been made, and the opinion of men who are in the best position to form well-founded conclusions appears to be practically unanimous that the productive capacity of the deep levels will prove not less than that of the companies working on the outcrop itself, while it may prove much greater.

At this moment there are fifty-three companies working on the outcrop claims. They employ 3370 white men and 32,100 natives, and they are producing gold at the rate of £4,500,000 sterling per annum. And these figures are only an approximation to the possible output from existing sources. Very few of the mines have attained to more than half their full legitimate production. Many are working with inadequate machinery and development, and on almost virgin property. Some are not at present contributing to the output at all, but are developing with a view to future results. Better methods of working, modern developments in the scientific treatment of ore, and cheapened transport, which will allow of the freer use of machinery, must steadily increase the total of production.

One particularly interesting element in the permanent sources of increase is the new departure which has lately been made in the chemical treatment of concentrates and tailings. Chlorination and cyanide works have been established, in which, by an ingenious and simple process, gold is melted by solution out of the powdered ore, just as sugar might be melted out of sawdust. A quantity of gold which used to be lost is in this way recovered, and goes to swell the average of production. The amount may be judged by the returns for May, which were the latest I was able to obtain. The ordinary mill returns gave 9.99 dwt. of gold per ton of ore produced, while gold recovered from all sources brought the average up to 12.3 dwt. per ton. The cyanide of potassium process has been so lately adopted that tailings are being produced eight times faster than they can at present be dealt with. The mass of accumulated tailings has, therefore, to be reckoned in the assets of the future.

The late depression in shares is another fact which is reckoned by the owners of mines as a cause of increase in the output. It has had the effect of sending underground managers, mining engineers, and others employed in the mines away from the speculative markets and back to their work, where during the boom it was next door to an impossibility to keep them. The result has been a considerable development, which is now showing fruit. Year by year since the first returns were made upon the Rand, in the middle of 1887, the figures of the output have shown a steady increase. For the first half-year up to the end of 1887 they were 23,155 oz.; in 1888, 208,121 oz.; in 1889, 369,557 oz.; in 1890, 494,817 oz.; in 1891, 729,338 oz.; and for the six months which have elapsed of 1892 the total returns have already reached 562,452 oz. There seems to be little doubt in the minds of the best men in Johannesburg that this increase might be expected to grow steadily. The opening of the railway will further so cheapen transport as to render possible the working of a number of low-grade reefs, which are at present considered unpayable, and if the views generally entertained with regard to the deep-level workings be correct, the basin of the Rand may be held to be only at the beginning of an unparalleled record of gold production.

The Witwatersrand is the best known, the best developed, and probably the richest of the gold-fields of the Transvaal, but there are still many others of which the capacities have been very imperfectly tested. The conglomerate beds of the Klerksdorp fields are of low grade, but they are large and regular, and they are precisely the sort of reef of which the working will profit by the cheapening of transport. Barberton, Lydenburg, Zoutpansberg, Middelburg, have all yielded returns which are not to be despised. In the Malmani, Potchefstroom, and Pretoria districts gold-mining is still only in its pioneer stage. Gold reefs occur in almost every part of the country, and, though the unreliability of the rotten quartz lodes of Lydenburg and the gash and fissure mines of Barberton and other districts has strengthened the belief that in this country conglomerate beds alone can support a really great gold industry, no one can say with assured conviction that another Rand may not any day be opened to development. Gold does not labour under the disadvantage of diamonds, that over-production is likely to lessen its value appreciably in the markets of the world. The Transvaal offers, therefore, a practically unlimited field of enterprise in this direction.

Next to gold comes the silver industry. Already

the question of its development takes rank in the questions which interest Johannesburg with the development of the deep levels of the Rand. They are two great mining questions of the immediate future. Silver zones extend over about 1500 square miles of country in the Pretoria and Middelburg districts. Some of the lodes are large and of very high grade. They have been opened up to a depth of 300 feet, and have been proved to have an average mineral contents of 25 per cent of lead and 30 oz. of silver per ton. The shipments which have been made have proved highly profitable, but only the best ores can stand the cost of transport and shipping. Silver-mining as an industry must, therefore, depend upon local treatment. The first smelting on a large scale will take place this month,[1] and the result is looked for with great interest as well as confidence. With beds so rich and so extensive there is little doubt of the ultimate result, but profitable development may have to wait, like that of other industries, for the opening of the railway.

It is difficult to imagine as yet how great a difference the opening of railway communication will make to the development of the Transvaal. The country waits for it, as a forest when the sap is rising waits for the spring sunshine to bring it into leaf. Gold and silver, by their precious quality in small bulk, appeal to the imagination, and a country which is rich in them is at once reckoned among the rich places of the earth. But in the opinion of many capitalists the working of these metals only touches the fringe of the real mineral wealth which is waiting for development. Iron and copper will, it

[1] Written in July 1892.

is thought, form the staple of mining industry when facilities of transport have made it possible to work them at a profit. The quantities which exist are sufficient to give employment to successive generations long after every scrap of now prospected gold and silver has been taken from the ground.

The country also teems with coal. Coal-fields divide and partly encircle the gold and silver regions. In the neighbourhood of Bohsberg coal, which is the later formation, overlies the gold, the two formations having actually been struck in the same shaft. This coal is not of good quality, but at Brakpan colliery, 20 miles by rail from Johannesburg, good steam-coal is turned out at the rate of 16,000 tons monthly. At a vertical depth of 90 feet the seam is 25 feet thick, and extends for some miles. The Brakpan pit is within a few hundred yards of some of the best mines on the eastern end of the Rand. On the Vaal River, surrounding the present terminus of the Cape railway, there is an extensive coal-field of still better class; and at the Oliphant River pits, which, notwithstanding 50 miles of road transport, at present supply Johannesburg with gas and coking-coal, a coal is obtained which is esteemed to be nearly equal to the best imported.

Almost the whole of the plateau known as the High Veldt contains huge coal deposits, and in the Heidelburg, Middelburg, Pretoria, Ermelo, and Wakkerstroom districts, down to the borders of Swaziland and Natal, there are thousands of square miles of coal-beds, of which the value is utterly unknown. The mere fact that at Cape Town coal for domestic purposes costs at present £3 : 12s. a ton, and that at Kimberley the price has been known to mount to

£9 a ton, is enough to illustrate the possible value of the Transvaal beds. Many other minerals, such as cobalt, asbestos, cinnabar, etc., occur in various districts.

Never was there a country to which the saying of Job could be more suggestively applied: "Surely there is a vein for the silver, and a place for gold where they fine it. Iron is taken out of the earth, and brass is molten out of the stone. . . . As for the earth, out of it cometh bread." In Johannesburg, whether you will or not, you must take interest in the details of mining enterprise. Your ears are filled with them from morning to night. Men who have been successful in the past are confident of the future, and the place literally simmers with the energy of fresh undertakings. You are no sooner well out of the town than your attention is drawn, with scarcely less overwhelming evidence, to the agricultural possibilities of the soil.

Between Johannesburg and Pretoria, on either side of the line of the future railway, there lies a farm of which the fence measures 24 miles round. The extent of it includes mountain-tops and water-levels. Scientific farming has only been attempted upon it within the last two years, and if I were to endeavour to describe the full result I should probably be accused of wishing to re-edit *Robinson Crusoe*. Everything that is written of the material resources of this astonishing country must read like exaggeration, and yet exaggeration is hardly possible. The fertility of the soil is no less amazing than the mineral wealth. The farm of which I speak lies on the northern slopes of the descent from Johannesburg —northern having, of course, in this hemisphere the signification of southern in our own. Its valleys have, therefore, every advantage of sunny and sheltered situation, and it is scarcely too much to say that it includes within its fence all the climates of the temperate world. The hill-tops have been planted with European forest trees — pine, oak, chestnut, etc. ; the lower slopes are clothed with vines ; and in the valleys plantations of oranges and lemons alternate with American, Australian, and African timber.

There is hardly a crop from tea to turnips which I did not see in the course of a long morning's drive. Among them were the *Pyrethrum persicum*, better known to fame in the form of Keating's insect powder, and the pea-nut, of which the pretty habits of growth and the profitable nature as an article of consumption were alike unknown to me. Another specially African crop were the varieties of watermelon, which are grown for feeding cattle, and of which fields still lay ripening in the sun. It was, however, a little late for them, as the plants die down under the first frosts, which are usually felt about the middle of May.

Winter is accounted to last here from the 15th of May to the 15th of August, and during those months there is little or no rain. The remaining nine months of the year are summer months, during which the rainfall is plentiful and regular. Most European cereals and roots yield more than one crop in the year. Wheat, rye, and barley are sown in April, May, June, July, and reaped in September, October, and November. Oats are sown the whole year round, but only rust-proof varieties in the summer. Potatoes are planted every month from

August until February. Those planted in August, September, and October are ripe and can be used for seed to be planted from December to January. Swedish turnips, mangold-wurzel, beets, carrots, onions, peas, and all varieties of the cabbage family are sown and reaped the whole year round. The native crops of maize, millet, sorghum, broom-corn, sweet-corn, etc., are sown from August to January. Sowing and reaping go on all the year side by side and there is no fallow time for the ground.

The best illustration is a mere list of the crops which I noted on either side as we drove down one avenue alone; it is to be remembered that we were nearly in mid-winter. There were pea-nuts ready for reaping and green oats, barley in the ear and barley in the shoot, Swedish turnips fit for storing and Swedish turnips just shooting, mangold-wurzel also in both stages, rye in the ear, carrots quite young and carrots ready for storing, potatoes in both stages; and in one immense field the sowers and the reapers had literally met. At the far end maize was standing, reapers were busy cutting and carrying the sheaves of corn, upon their heels sowers followed putting wheat into the ground, and at the near end, where, my host told me, maize had been standing ten days before, thin green blades of wheat were already shooting.

So vigorous is the growth of everything, that forest trees planted only two years ago were already high enough to give shade; apples grown from seed of March and grafted in October will bear fruit this year. With the exception of cherries, gooseberries, and currants, all European fruits flourish well. Throughout the estate the watercourses which divided the fields were bordered by hedges of quince, pear, apple, plum, and peach. The gardens contained a profusion of European vegetables and fruit trees. Acres of roses, violets, and ornamental plants surrounded the house, but nothing seemed to impress upon me more vividly the rapidity with which the place had sprung into being than the simple fact that after hours of driving through vineyards, woods, and cornfields we were met at the door of the house by a baby child of two and a half who was older than everything that we had seen. The estate had been named after her. When she was born the spot on which it stands was nothing but bare veldt.

The idea occurs at once that this farm may have been an exception. So it is in the matter of development, for the Transvaal farms are, as a rule, cattle farms upon which little or no agriculture in the modern sense is carried on. But I am told that it forms no exception whatever in the matter of soil and climate. Land near the future railway is valuable, but the owner of the farm assured me that land equally fertile may be obtained in almost any other part of the Transvaal at the cost of a few shillings an acre. Land companies are buying it up; timber companies are planting it, and the spread of lines of communication will rapidly raise its value. A good many fortunes will no doubt be lost as well as made in speculation with it.

But wherever there is wealth to develop speculation is only the forerunner of genuine enterprise; and seeing such a soil in one of the very best climates of the world, with a mining population pouring in to create markets on the spot, it is impossible to escape from the conviction that the phenomenon which you witness in the eager push of development all round is nothing less than a continent in the making. The natural resources are here, capital and energy have been brought to bear upon them, and the country appears to be opening by a principle of growth as simple and as irresistible as that which governs the opening of a rose in summer. Improvement in the material conditions is, of course, an essential part of the development.

At present, notwithstanding the agricultural possibilities of the neighbourhood, the price of food in Johannesburg and Pretoria is, with the one exception of meat, excessively high. A cauliflower in Johannesburg will cost as much as 3s., eggs are from 5s. to 6s. a dozen, a half-quartern loaf costs 1s., milk goes up to 1s. 6d. a quart, and butter to 5s. a pound. The farmer might be supposed to profit, but in the long run he does not, for the market is so unsteady that there are occasions when he finds it impossible to dispose of perishable produce at any price, and he never can count upon a regular demand. The consumer in self-defence trusts largely to tinned and imported food. Hence retaliatory endeavours on the one hand to impose prohibitive taxes upon food, and upon the other to obtain a Customs Union which would include in its advantages the right of free trade in food stuffs throughout South Africa.

The economic theories of the Dutch agriculturist are remarkable, and first among them ranks a belief that markets must be treated like French babies and closely swaddled to help their growth. The fact that a large proportion of French babies die under this process has not, so far as is generally known, destroyed the faith of their nurses in the system. Nor is the Dutch farmer a bit more naturally inclined to draw logical conclusions from his not dissimilar experience. A well-to-do Boer was one day boasting that he had obtained exactly double the price which he had expected for his wheat. "I suppose," an English friend said, congratulating him, "that you will sow a double quantity this year." "A double quantity?" replied the Dutchman; "half the quantity you mean! Don't you see that with a double price half the quantity will give me the same return?" The advent of the railway can alone do away with this kind of thing. Facilities of transport will tend to equalise and enlarge existing markets as well as to put the supply of the Transvaal in touch with the demand of the world. This done, it is scarcely to be conceived that Dutch producers should remain still unwilling to benefit by their wider opportunities. If they should, there is but one thing that can happen. They will find themselves exposed to the competition of foreigners who will settle upon the soil, and they will be forced, whether they will or no, to swim with the tide. The main fact is, that a tide is rising which promises to sweep obstacles of the Dame Partington kind irresistibly before it.

The Transvaal has been proved to be as valuable as Mr. Gladstone once thought it valueless, and nothing short of a convulsion can arrest the developing movement in which increasing numbers of men are every day finding their individual advantage. The most serious hindrance lies in the difficulty of obtaining labour, and it is a difficulty which, as I pointed out at Kimberley, has been only very partially surmounted by the application of the compound system to mining districts.

If I have filled my letter with details which give it rather the appearance of a catalogue than a description, it is because I want to support as far as possible with the argument of facts the conclusion that material development is the supreme interest of the country. Johannesburg as a town sits in the middle of this development, and to a great extent directs it. Already it has placed a great distance between itself and a mere mining camp, and is rapidly advancing to the position which it desires to take as the Manchester or Birmingham of South Africa. That it has done as much as it has without any connected line of communication is an earnest of the growth which may be expected after the railway has placed it upon the highways of the world. The opportunities which it offers are very great, and there is nothing to wonder at in the fact that able and successful men who are gradually gathering the development of productive enterprise into their hands find a vitality in their daily work with which they say that nothing in London or the other European centres can compare. These are the men who represent the progressive life of the place.

The worthless and unscrupulous speculator who has made Johannesburg a byword of crooked ways exists, of course, but it would be unjust not to recognise that he exists as a parasite upon a better growth. I think it may fairly be said that everything which is not material development is mere excrescence. The conditions of social life are for the most part frankly detestable. It is an opinion in which I have no fear that the better portion of Johannesburg society will not cordially agree. But they are not worth writing about. They must evidently change—are changing in fact—with the changing future; and in relation to the future the enormous wealth of the country has such a preponderating importance that the course which the development of that wealth is likely to follow absorbs all serious attention. The whole political situation hangs upon the material situation. But I hope to show this more clearly in a letter from Pretoria.

IV

PRETORIA.

PRETORIA as it is first seen lying in a ford of the veldt at the foot of the Johannesburg slopes, with its white houses embosomed in trees and gardens, divided each from the other by blossoming rose hedges, has all the character of the capital of a pastoral Republic. As you approach and enter the streets you find that its changing position as the political centre of a new and rapidly-growing country is no less faithfully expressed. The first object which struck my eye was a big placard announcing in English that an auction of farm-stock would be held on the following Thursday. A few steps farther on another English advertisement gave notice of a political meeting. In the first street of shops, bootmakers and haberdashers, stationers and butchers, declared their trades in English; announcements of sales, assurances of bargains, were all posted up in English.

Evidently the public whom these things concerned was English. At the hotel the coloured servants spoke in English, and dinner hour filled the dining-rooms with Englishmen. I had occasion to seek out a friend whose address I did not know. In the course of a morning's drive, inquiring at perhaps twenty houses, though my companion, who was a native of the place, served as the medium of communication, there was not one house in which English was not the common language. The first Dutch words which I heard spoken in Pretoria were in the house of President Kruger, and a hasty impression might lead to the belief that the only Dutch things in the town are its President and Council.

This impression is far from being literally accurate. The Boer population of the Republic has its fitting representation here. Dutch feeling and Dutch habits of life and thought are the substratum upon which the town exists, and Dutch character is too sturdy and tenacious to allow itself to be easily carried away in the foreign stream. But in relation to what may be called the New Transvaal—that is, the Transvaal of the modern mining development, the Transvaal which is taking its place in the competition of the world—the impression is near enough to the truth to be accepted as at least typifying the actual state of affairs. The pastoral Transvaal is Dutch. The industrial Transvaal, actually cosmopolitan, is practically an English state presided over by a Dutch government. That these two Transvaals should be so intimately intermingled as to have no geographical dividing lines, does not alter the fact that the two exist within the frontiers traced by the Vaal and Limpopo rivers.

At present the English Transvaal concerns itself very little with politics. It is too busy with the work it has undertaken. Time enough when theories of government affect the business of development to have opinions about them. A President who puts obstacles in the way of the mining industry will be roughly hooted at Johannesburg. A President who grants running powers to a Cape and Free State Railway will be cheered and received with flags and triumphal arches. He is one and the same man. No matter! The President is nothing to them; they want mining facilities and cheap transport, and take their own impolite, vigorous way of expressing the fact. Their concern is with the world rather than with the Transvaal. Yet they form part of the Transvaal, and as they follow their rough progressive road, they drag it half-unconsciously along with them. Briefly, their affairs may be said to constitute the foreign politics of the Republic, but they are generally content to leave them in other hands. The affairs of their pastoral neighbours are the home affairs to which newcomers are still too strange to give a thought. But it is perfectly evident that home and foreign affairs cannot remain distinct, nor the old and the new Republics exist for ever within the same frontier without becoming interfused.

The question of the future is under what conditions this fusion of interests will take place. There are people who regard the two forces as necessarily antagonistic. For them it resolves itself into the simpler question of which is to dominate the other. But looked at in a broader light it is possible to think that, before the day of domination comes for either, the interests of both are likely to be identical. We have a parallel to this position at home, in the apparently opposed yet intimately united interests of the Liberals of the manufacturing centres and the Tory landowners of the counties; and as there is not a man of either of the great English parties who does not feel that the welfare of England is his individual welfare, so it may be believed that before many years are past there will not be a man of either of the two Transvaals who will not feel that the good of the whole is his first and most intimate necessity. It may be said that the position is not parallel, because at home the nationality of both parties is the same, while here you have not only two parties but two peoples.

The new element in the situation is that this is a country in the making. Its parts are not yet welded together. We are assisting at the very interesting process, and nothing impresses itself more vividly as a result of watching it upon the spot than the futility of stirring questions of sentimental politics in the face of the overwhelming movement which is taking place. The operation of natural causes is all in favour of a successful issue. Let events take their course. The one thing to which they point unmistakably is the creation of an enormously rich province in South Africa. This is no less advantageous to South Africa than it is to the Republic itself, and since the increase of development in the Transvaal is synonymous with the increase of English influence there can be no doubt, so far as the strictly English part of the position is concerned, that English interest is to support and encourage the new development in every possible way. The natural wealth is Dutch, the energy to develop it is English, the profits of the whole will be

South African. It is almost an ideal situation if it can be protected from accident and left to the laws of its inherent evolution.

Unfortunately this is a great deal to ask. It means the sacrifice of prejudices on every side, and, furthermore, it presupposes that, even in this early stage of their coexistence, the wants and desires of the Old Transvaal are never to clash with the requirements of the New. The New Transvaal has no history and no sentiment. It has the present situation, and intends to make its history in the future. The three essential conditions to making it successfully are peace, facilities of transport, and better labour. If it can get these it wants nothing else.

But with the Old Transvaal the position is different. The Old Transvaal has its history, a vivid history which men of the last generation sacrificed everything to make and some of the present generation have fought and died for. It has its inheritance of sentiment stronger than any logic of self-interest, and there are points upon which, no matter what the consequences, its burghers take their stand behind their rifles and say, in the old Lutheran phrase, "We can no otherwise." To suppose that it can see without jealousy the new English Transvaal growing rapidly in its midst is to suppose the impossible. It may be for the ultimate good of the Republic that its resources should be utilised; but there is scarcely a farmer in the whole population who does not dread and resent the finding of payable minerals upon his farm. The anecdotes which abound with regard to their conduct when the fear is realised and minerals are found have their touching as well as their comic side. Corn and stock, not gold and silver, constitute their wealth. If a man can sell his farm and move on, well and good; trekking enters into their customs and costs them little.

But "moving on" grows more and more difficult every day. Where are they to move to? They look round them. South and west there is no issue. Northward? They used to think, not many years ago, that there across the Limpopo lay a limitless field in which their instinct of expansion might find play for generations yet to come. But their President —the man whom they themselves have chosen for their head—has entered into a compact with England by which he binds himself and them never to extend the frontier beyond the river. England is filling that country which they had vaguely thought of as theirs. They fall back like caged animals upon themselves and the farms rendered hateful to them by the sound of pick and stamp battery close at hand, and turn their faces eastward towards the sea. Out that way beyond the mountains, out that way towards the world, their appetite for space and freedom may be gratified. They have, after all, the blood of old Holland in their veins. The land of the continent has been closed to them. They ask for a sea-gate. It is easy to understand. They see that England has surrounded them by a ring fence, that she has even made irruption in irrepressible form within the fence. They feel the danger that they may be stifled out of their national existence, and they want an air-hole. They think that it will be more possible to contend with the foreign influence that permeates their being if they have ships of their own upon the sea. It strikes the English observer as a natural but rather pathetic hope. They are too late. Other nations are too far ahead of them in the naval race. If war should break out in Europe they must trust to England to protect them. In peace that must inevitably happen to them which happens to all nations. Their commercial navy will be the possession of their merchant princes—that is to say, of the very New Transvaal against whose supremacy its creation is now designed to strike a blow.

It is not, therefore, without significance that the Dutch language should have first greeted me at President Kruger's door. In crossing his threshold I entered the region of Dutch sentiment. There was nothing of which he wished to speak to me except the Swazi question, and upon this he put his views very frankly and forcibly before me.

"We feel," he said, "that we have a right to Swaziland. It belonged to us before England took the Transvaal. Had the Transvaal remained English, Swaziland would have remained an integral part of the country. Because the Transvaal was given back to the Dutch England separated the two and retained the annex. Is it of any use to her? None!"

He recapitulated the arguments arising from the geographical position of the Swazi country, and the great difficulty, amounting almost to impossibility, of approaching it from any English frontier.

"The Amatonga swamps and the Lebombo mountains give it to us. I have only to refer you to the report of your own Commissioner, Sir Francis de Winton, for our arguments. I desire no better statement of our case. He shows you what is the truth, that not only it ought to be ours, but, as a matter of fact, it already is ours in all but name. We hold all the valuable concessions, and we have all the practical expenses of administration. The right to build railways, the roads, the posts, the telegraphs—all State rights are in our hands. You could not take these over without incurring an expenditure much greater than they involve to us, because to us Swaziland, surrounded as it is on three sides by the Transvaal, represents merely an extension of our own system; to you it would represent the creation of a separate system at many hundreds of miles from your nearest base. We are glad for the sake of our own people to do what we do for it under present circumstances.

"The grazing rights are all held and enjoyed by Boers, who naturally desire to remain under their own Government. The natives look to us, and are constantly asking to be taken under our protection. Historically, geographically, administratively, it is ours. All this being so—admitted so by English as well as by Dutch statements of the case—you will understand the strong feeling with which the Dutch people asks, 'Why is it kept from us?' It is kept by right of the strongest, not to do yourselves good, but to do us harm. Well, if we were dangerous to you the argument might have some force. But who are we? What can we do? Can we rival England? Can we even injure England? You are afraid to give us a seaport! Can our two or three ships upon the sea upset the balance of the first Navy of the world? England, who has everything to gain by working with us! Show me what it is that she fears from us?"

I suggested the possibility of some future President of the Transvaal seeking to ally himself with a foreign Power, and to introduce a foreign influence into South Africa.

"With England surrounding us on three sides by land, with English railways able to place English troops upon our frontier, with English ships upon the sea? Impossible! The work of England and the Transvaal in South Africa is the same work." Clasping his hands vigorously, he turned to me, "We ought to be working together thus," showing the interlaced fingers and palms pressed one to another. "Instead we are doing this"—and he struck one forefinger across the other—"hindering, not helping, the development which is good alike for all. You think that if I had a port I might give encouragement and preference to foreigners. It is nonsense! England, if she will but treat me fairly, shall have the preference always. I personally sympathise with her, because she is the only country which has the same religious spirit as the Transvaal. But if it were not so I must, for reasons of interest, still give her every preference. I give you my word that I ask nothing better than to work with England as a younger brother might work with his elder. I desire to be in amity and in profitable relations with the greatest power in South Africa, but I will not work with her as a slave. If I would I could not. Our spirit as a people is too much like the English spirit. It is stronger than us; it masters any advantage that we might gain, and forces us to maintain our independence."

He spoke with a rugged emotion, which had its own peculiar force, and from all that I have been able to learn his representation of the feeling of the people is strictly true. An essential difference between the Old Transvaal and the New Transvaal is that the Old Transvaal is ready, if necessary, to fight, and the New Transvaal is not. "And now can you wonder," he continued, "that we feel sore when we find that a Government as strong and prosperous as the English Government, a Government with which all our best interests incline us to work harmoniously, can condescend to trick and quibble with us, and time after time take the advantage of our mutual agreements, yet hold back the price for which we made them?"

This is not the place in which to attempt an exposition of the whole Swazi question, but in order that the feeling of President Kruger and his people may be understood, it is necessary to indicate very briefly the course of its later developments. The convention of 1884 bound both England and the Transvaal to respect the independence of Swaziland. The same convention bound the Transvaal not to enlarge its northern border. No measures were taken to enforce the observance of these conditions, and, as a matter of fact, the Boers of the Transvaal spread both into Swaziland and across the Limpopo northwards, where they explored and made treaties with the chiefs.

When the British South Africa Company obtained its charter it became necessary to take note of the informal extension of Dutch influence to the north. Swaziland was at the same time rapidly falling into anarchy. Sir Francis de Winton was sent to Swaziland, and made his report upon the condition of affairs. It was informally understood that it would be an arrangement satisfactory to all sides if Swaziland were handed over to the Transvaal, and in return the Transvaal should renounce any advantage which it might have obtained under treaties with native chiefs towards the north, where it should give all its influence and support to the chartered company. The arrangement was not carried out. President Kruger was informed that it was not considered desirable that Swaziland should pass immediately under the sole sway of the Republic, and the present system of joint jurisdiction was temporarily established.

It will be remembered that opinion in England was at that time very much divided as to the ultimate destination of Swaziland. Its cession to the Transvaal was advocated in the Press as late as the month of February of 1890. It is not surprising that the Government of the Transvaal, fresh from the impression of Sir Francis de Winton's report, believed that at the expiration of the term fixed for the temporary government the country would be formally transferred to it. At a meeting between the President and the High Commissioner at Blignaut's Pont in March this hope was destroyed. A draft convention, which reaffirmed the independence of the Swazi people, was reluctantly accepted by President Kruger, subject to the approval of his Council. The Council refused to ratify his acceptance, and by the middle of the year the position had become so strained that war was on the point of breaking out. Rifle practice became a regular institution among the Boers in Swaziland. An English police force was understood to be in readiness to cross the frontier. Natives were preparing to range themselves upon either side. It was at this crisis that Mr. Hofmeyr was induced to undertake his mission to Pretoria as special agent of Her Britannic Majesty.

Mr. Hofmeyr has rendered many services to the Empire. None is deserving of more grateful recognition than that which he rendered by saving us in the summer of 1890 from another African campaign. War would not only have put an end with its first shot to the policy of conciliation between the Dutch and English inhabitants of South Africa, to which Mr. Hofmeyr has consecrated the labours of his own public life; it would have been disastrous to the material development of the country, and have thrown back for, perhaps, another generation the chances of that peaceable expansion which is the complement of conciliation.

It is probable that the English public will never realise all that it owes him in this respect, because it can never know how close and real the peril was. He arrived in Pretoria in the last days of June. He had to achieve the difficult and delicate task of negotiating the acceptance of a distasteful convention, in the provisions of which it must have been well known from his public utterances upon the subject that he did not himself heartily concur. He succeeded by force of the same directness of purpose and simplicity of action which have made his name respected in all camps of politicians in the colony. He took the convention himself as a compromise. He induced the Transvaal Government to accept it in the same spirit. Diplomacy would have been useless. He laid it aside and spoke the plain truth to the President. He put him face to face with the consequences of war. He pointed out to him that England could not afford to have another Majuba, and that war must mean nothing less than the wiping of the Transvaal off the map. The arguments of sentiment were ruthlessly met by arguments of fact. At the same time he admitted the strength of the Dutch case, and the Government of Pretoria was given to understand that if the proposed arrangement were temporarily accepted a modification of it in the direction desired by the Transvaal would afterwards be favourably entertained by Her Majesty's Government.

The understanding was entered into verbally, and a memorandum of it was embodied in the third clause of an authorised communication which Mr. Hofmeyr made to President Kruger on 17th July. The wording of the clause is as follows: " Her Majesty's Government will be prepared, when the joint Government is established and concession claims are settled, to consider such questions as the Government of the South African Republic may bring before it with a desire to meet the wishes of the South African Republic as far as possible." The Dutch Government, having verbally explained that the question which they would bring before Her Majesty's Government would be the cession of Swaziland, were anxious to give weight to this communication by inserting it as an article of the convention. This was refused by Mr. Hofmeyr on the ground that in his letter of 17th July "the Dutch Government already possessed the written promise of Her Majesty's Government, and that should be accepted as sufficient guarantee that the obligations will be acknowledged."

The Dutch Blue Book which contains this correspondence contains also a further despatch from the High Commissioner, in which he guarantees the signature of Mr. Hofmeyr as binding. The convention was signed at Pretoria on the 2nd of August. The Transvaal obtained under its terms the right to acquire a seaport at Kosi Bay, and bound itself to abstain from any attempt to extend its frontier to the north.

These details are a little tedious, but necessary, in order to show the ground upon which the Government of the Transvaal base the very sore and bitter feeling that is entertained. There may be, of course, a difference of opinion as to how much was conceded by the verbal understanding that underlay the claim in question. There can be no doubt of the construction which the Dutch Government puts upon it. "This," President Kruger said to me in summing up the situation, "is how we regard the matter. Great Britain, in the person of her representative, refused to enter into a bond with us, but gave us the word of a gentleman. We accepted that word. We fulfilled our part of the bargain upon trust, and the word has not been kept. We have no redress. There is nothing in the bond to show what our expectations were, but the Swazi question now bars the way to all hearty co-operation with English schemes—first, by the irritation which it causes; secondly, by the fact that so long as that which we hold to be a promise is unredeemed it is not possible to put faith in any promise made by England. Treaties are in the nature of things invalidated beforehand."

To this it may be replied that there is evidently a misunderstanding as to their conception of what the British Government undertook to do, and as for the rest the convention of 1890 gives them practically all they want. It recognises the principal concessions which they hold; it leaves them undisturbed in the possession of their grazing rights; it gives them power to acquire a seaport, and agrees to recognise the sovereignty of the South African Republic in respect of land purchased from the native rulers of the coast for the purpose of constructing a railway to the sea. They have the nut. Why are they so anxious for the nutshell? I venture to put the argument the other way. Since we have given them the nut, why do we quarrel for the nutshell? Every solid advantage which it was once feared to grant has been conceded. All that remains to us is an expensive and irksome responsibility for an unhealthy country, into which, in the event of a disturbance, there is, in Sir Hercules Robinson's words, no entrance for our troops but by balloon. Is this worth retaining at the cost of a standing irritation between ourselves and an otherwise friendly neighbour? The English situation in the Transvaal is good enough. Suppose the construction of a harbour. Suppose the creation of a navy. Suppose every form of satisfactory development in the Dutch Republic. Who will benefit by it?

If I have succeeded in these two letters in showing anything it must be that we have only to maintain friendly relations with the Transvaal, and there is no gain of hers which will not be also a gain of ours. There is no reason why we should wish to overpower her Government or to cramp her growth. Our interests are in the best sense united, and if we can but pocket old-fashioned red rags, and confine ourselves to the development of industrial and other enterprise in which the lead is granted to us without a question, the next generation of Englishmen will have no reason to complain of the situation which will have been created for them in South Africa. What English supremacy demands is not the destruction of other Governments nor the suppression of other individualities. There is room for all these under her wing. It is railway development, customs union, gradual modification of other conditions which now impede the current of expansion, above all, an increased white population. Political convulsion can only hinder the attainment of these ends, and, if the day has not yet arrived in which our swords may be safely beaten into ploughshares, South Africa can claim to have reached at least a preliminary stage in which the steam-engine has become a more effective instrument of empire than the cannon.

V

BLOEMFONTEIN.

As the train rolls over the monotonous stretches of veldt which lie between Bloemfontein and the frontier of the Orange Free State, you have time to meditate upon the changes which are likely to be produced in such a country as this by the introduction of modern means of locomotion. From sunrise to sunset the prospect remains the same. On all sides a yellow plain of grass, overhead a blue plain of sky, not a tree, not an eminence of any kind to break the distant meeting line, only here and there between the two a swarm of locusts, fluttering snow-white if the sun be upon them, and here and there ant-heaps in regular rows, which look as if they had been prepared for some agricultural purpose. Cattle browse upon the grass. Occasionally there is a farm, still more rarely a village. From time to time the course of a distant stream may be traced by the greener line of herbage and brushwood which it marks upon the plain. Otherwise through the long hours there is no change. The eyes open in the morning upon the prospect on which they closed at night.

The distances, with nothing to mark them, seem immense, and imagination recoils from the endeavour even to conceive the patience required for traversing them without the aid of steam. Yet there is something in the mild wide landscape which reminds you irresistibly of the " trekker " in his white-tented wagon whom you passed at the beginning of your journey in the Karoo. Here you feel is the goal to which he travelled; it is the true home of the ox wagon. Here the animals can obtain fodder and the driver meat. Here there is room for every man to put the wide space which he desires between himself and his neighbour. Here is essentially the Dutchman's country.

The Orange Free State is absolutely an inland State. The shortest distance that lies between its frontier and the Indian Ocean is 150 miles, and on the other side the Orange River, after it leaves the border, has still a course of 500 miles to run before it reaches the Atlantic. The mountains of Natal, Basutoland, and the eastern districts of Cape Colony enclose it on the south and east, and shut from it even so much as a sea-wind. The veldt is its only ocean, and this until two years ago had been crossed by no vessel but a wagon.

From the foot of the mountains the Free State slopes gently towards the north—that is, towards the equator and the sun. It always maintains an average elevation of about 5000 feet above the sea, and it contains within its lozenge-shaped frontier 72,000 square miles, or an area about a third of the size of France, of scarcely broken plains which are swept by the dry desert air. Its climate is hardly to be matched throughout the world. In the absence of salt water it is almost entirely surrounded by fresh water. The Klip Vaal, Caledon and Orange Rivers form a natural moat along at least five-sixths of its boundary. Other small streams traverse it from south to north. None of the land remains now unowned, but the population averages rather less than two persons—one white and one black—to the square mile, almost the whole of it being South African born. With few exceptions, such as the diamonds at Fauresmith, the minerals have not been worked. It is a purely pastoral and agricultural State, and the possibilities of development which lie before it are practically untested. This is the history of all internal States until easy means of communication have been opened for them with the world, and at Bloemfontein, which entered upon a new state of being when the railway reached it eighteen months ago, the question of communications is now regarded as the question of supreme importance.

It does not need the memory of an old man to recall the time when not only Bloemfontein but the whole peninsula was without a single line of rail. Thirty years ago private companies were only beginning to grasp the necessity for developing the country from the seaports, and the first South African railway between Cape Town and Wellington was not opened until 1863. Another line from Port Elizabeth to Uitenhage was begun by a private company, but when the Government took over the railways in 1873 there were only 63 miles of railway open in the country. Since that time more than 2000 miles have been constructed, and the traffic over them pays interest of $4\frac{2}{3}$ per cent upon a capital of £16,500,000. This is exclusive of the railways of Natal, which do not yet form a part of the Cape and Free State system.

The first policy of the Government after taking over the existing lines was to push them from the coast into the cultivated districts of the near neighbourhood. The Cape Town line was advanced to Beaufort, and the Port Elizabeth line to Cradock on the one branch and Graaf Reinet upon the other, before any decision was taken as to the ultimate point of junction. A third port line was opened from East London to King William's Town in 1877. Brandy, wool, skins, and feathers were the principal markets which the lines were designed to serve. It was supposed that they would some day converge upon a given point in the interior, but it was not until the discovery of diamonds at Kimberley and the addition of Griqualand West to the colonial territory that the Kimberley trade leaped into sudden importance, and Kimberley became the goal of all the railways. A point of junction was chosen at De Aar for the Cape Town and Cradock lines, and a main line was pushed on from there to the Orange River, whence, in consequence of Sir Charles Warren's expedition in 1885, it was continued into Kimberley. The East London line was in the meantime extended to Aliwal North, upon the borders of the Free State. Thus the system within the colony itself was completed, and local opposition on the part of the more conservative farming population, which was at one time strong, became a thing of the past.

There was, however, no connection between the colony and the neighbouring Republics, and discoveries of gold in the Transvaal were already, by the time the railway had reached Kimberley, beginning to draw trade as the diamonds had done.

All eyes looked towards Johannesburg. The question for the directors of South African railway construction was how to tap its trade at the nearest point. In 1882 a concession had been granted by the Government of the Transvaal to the Netherlands South African Railway Company to construct a railway from the borders of Portuguese territory on the eastern coast into Pretoria, but, in consequence of difficulties with Colonel M'Murdo, the concessionaire for the construction of the line through Portuguese territory to the sea at Delagoa Bay, nothing had been done. The Transvaal, therefore, was without any railway of its own, and seemed likely to remain so for an indefinite period. The prize lay between the two English colonies, and Natal had already built a line to Ladysmith, about 190 miles inland.

Railway extension passed at this point from a question of local advantage to a question of South African politics. All parties desired it. The division of opinion was upon the manner in which it should be carried out. In consequence of the deadlock which had taken place in his own railway extension in the Transvaal, President Kruger refused his consent to any immediate extension of colonial lines into his territory. He could not, of course, forbid either Natal or the Cape to extend their railways if they chose to the extreme limits of their territory and his. He could only lay before them his not unnatural dislike to see the trade of his own country taken away before his railway was constructed, and he asked them as a neighbourly act to give him a fair chance of competing for it by waiting until the difficulties with the Portuguese part of his line had been got over. He put his proposal in the form of a request that Natal would remain at Ladysmith and the Cape at Kimberley until the Netherlands Railway Company got upon the high veldt 120 miles from Delagoa Bay.

It is important to remember that Johannesburg, which is still, as it was then, the goal of the South African railway system, is 6000 feet above the sea. From whatever point of the coast it is reached this ascent has to be made. On the Delagoa Bay line, which is geographically the shortest of them all, there are portions where the gradient is 1 in 20, and to get the line upon the high veldt was equivalent to achieving the most difficult as well as the most costly part of the construction.

Natal, it may be briefly said, disregarded President Kruger's wish, and pushed on her Ladysmith line to Charlestown upon the Transvaal frontier. In the Cape Parliament in 1888 Sir Gordon Sprigg's Government proposed a scheme of extending each of the three Cape lines as far as they could be carried to the borders respectively of the Free State and the Transvaal. The part of the scheme which involved extension to the Transvaal frontier was strenuously opposed by Mr. Hofmeyr and the majority of his party, who declared themselves in favour of respecting President Kruger's wish, and of carrying on the Cape railway system by extension into the Free State. The scheme was carried, but in the following session, in deference, it was supposed, to the drift of the general election which took place between the sessions of 1888-89, Sir Gordon Sprigg abandoned the extension to the Transvaal frontier and adopted the policy indicated by Mr. Hofmeyr. He concluded a

Customs Union with the Free State and entered into a convention to build the railway as far as Bloemfontein.

This convention was subject to an agreement entered into between the Presidents of the two Republics at Potchefstroom that the railway should not be carried further than Bloemfontein without the consent of President Kruger. About the same time the British South Africa Company got its charter, and the Kimberley line was, by arrangement, extended to Vryburg. Sir Gordon Sprigg's Ministry was defeated in the early part of the session of 1890 upon a scheme of railway development within the Colony, and the present Government took office. The Vryburg and Bloemfontein extensions were both of them completed in December of 1890, thus creating the basis of the two future trunk lines of South Africa—the one from Cape Town to join the Netherlands railway line in Pretoria, and so gain an issue by Delagoa Bay, connecting as it goes the two Republics, and possibly some day Natal; the other within British territory, to push up probably by degrees as far as British territory may extend throughout the continent, and to gather on its way all branch lines running east and west, beginning with the line about to be constructed from Beira to Fort Salisbury.

The destiny of the Vryburg line is still a question of the future; the Bloemfontein line has fulfilled in great part the intention with which it was constructed. The opening of the railway in 1890 gave the Free State a new standing in South Africa. Its wishes and its affairs became at once of more importance, and every one now sees, what in 1888

Mr. Hofmeyr alone was astute enough to recognise, that its influence with the Transvaal was worth winning. Incidentally the result achieved in this matter of railway extension may be taken as one of the fruits of the policy of conciliation. While the Natal railway still remains at Charlestown, 180 miles from the point which it desires to reach, the Cape and Free State railway is on the point of entering Johannesburg. A Cape railway alone might have remained, like the Natal railway, to this day upon the frontier of the Transvaal at Fourteen Streams, further even than Charlestown from Johannesburg, for we have not done much to dispose President Kruger towards friendly concessions to us personally.

We owe our present favourable position in large measure to our friendship with the Free State. President Reitz was naturally desirous of obtaining for the Free State agriculturists as large a share as possible of the produce trade with Johannesburg, and the extension was scarcely completed to Bloemfontein when President Kruger was induced to sanction a further development through the Free State to the frontier of the Transvaal at Vereeniging, a distance of only 50 miles from Johannesburg.

In December of 1891, in return for a loan made by the Cape Government to the Netherlands Railway Company for the purpose of constructing the line from the frontier to Johannesburg and Pretoria, running powers into both those towns were granted to the trains of the Cape and Free State line. The extension to the frontier was opened on the 26th of May of this year, and it is expected that the first train will run into Johannesburg and Pretoria in the middle of September. In the meantime the Delagoa Bay line has advanced to Nels Spruit upon the high veldt, about 150 miles from Delagoa Bay, and Natal, seeing that the way to the Transvaal lies, after all, through the Free State, has also extended her railway to Harrismith, upon the Free State border.

It has been a sharp struggle, in which the sagacity and the command of capital of the Cape have established her position as the premier State of South Africa ; and the only matter of regret is that the rivalry which it has engendered between two English colonies should continue. Even this, perhaps, is not altogether a matter of regret, for rivalry, under judicious guidance, may tone down to wholesome competition, by which in the long run the public of the South will benefit. One of the conditions of the Cape agreement with the Transvaal is a personal promise from President Kruger that no better terms than those which have been granted to the Cape shall be given to any other Power which extends its railways into the Republic. This has been construed into an unfair and unfriendly attempt to debar Natal from extending its lines in due course. As a matter of fact, it is not so. It is nothing more than a parallel to the most favoured nation clause of any treaty, and was necessary for purposes of legitimate self-protection.

The immediate effect with regard to the extension of the Natal line from Charlestown would, however, be to weight goods carried over it with the same rate per mile that they pay upon the Cape railway from the point at which it enters the territory of the Republic. This rate is 6d. per ton. The distance

from the point of entrance of the Cape railway at
Vereeniging to Johannesburg is 52 miles. The
total cost for each ton of goods is therefore 26s.
The distance from Charlestown to Johannesburg is
180 miles. The total cost for each ton of goods
would be 90s., and this, added to the cost of carrying
them to Charlestown over a line of which the
gradients are very steep, is practically prohibitive.
The Cape line could always deliver the same goods
from Port Elizabeth or East London at a lower
price.

The scheme of a Charlestown extension is, therefore, likely for the present to be abandoned, but the
Harrismith extension through the Free State remains.
Here Natal would, of course, desire to strike by the
shortest route across the Free State and join the
existing railway at Vereeniging. But the Free State
had to have its say. Its voice in such matters now
has weight. It has obtained the market which it
required for its own produce at Johannesburg. It
can afford to wait for further developments, but if a
railway is to be constructed over its territory, it
must be run for the purposes of the Free State as
well as of Natal. In order to do this, it must
traverse the agricultural districts of the east and
strike the existing railway not further north than
Kronstad — that is, with 90 miles to run upon
the Cape and Free State rails. In other words,
it must become a branch of the existing trunk
line.

The Natal Government has not yet expressed
its intentions with regard to its future course. It
had been hoped that the meeting of President
Reitz and Sir Charles Mitchell at the late opening

of the extension to Harrismith would have resulted in an understanding upon these and other questions between the two Governments, but the impression brought back from the meeting appears to be that Natal is waiting to watch the course of further developments in the Transvaal before coming to any decision. In the meantime it has shown a keen determination to compete by train and wagon with the train service of the Cape, and in order to do so it has celebrated the opening of the Harrismith extension by a reduction of its carrying rates. The Cape has retaliated by a corresponding reduction.

I have not yet been in Natal, and, therefore, wish to say as little as possible about the attitude of that colony in the matter. This, however, may be said without fear of contradiction, that Natal has depended largely upon the carrying trade for the security of her financial position. Any circumstances tending to destroy that trade would constitute a serious misfortune, and, in fighting against the advantage which the Cape has gained by pushing its railway into Johannesburg, Natal is struggling to retain what it conceives to be the natural advantage of its own geographical position. Durban, it contends, is nearer to Johannesburg than East London. Therefore, it must be able to put goods into Johannesburg more cheaply than East London can. Here comes in again the fact, all important when tariffs have to be fixed, that Johannesburg is 6000 feet above the sea.

The reply of Cape authorities to the Natal argument is that, although geographically nearer, Durban is topographically further than the Cape ports from the seat of the Transvaal trade. It is not always shorter to go up the face of a mountain than round the shoulder, and when locomotive power has to be paid for and interest calculated upon the expenses of railway construction it will be found, they say, that neither is it cheaper. Twenty miles of railway through the Drakensberg mountains, which the Natal lines have to cross, cost more than 100 miles across the Free State.

I have no personal knowledge of the financial position of the Natal railways. The Cape railways contribute, as the Treasurer-General pointed out in his Budget speech, little less than half the public revenue. The capital which is invested in them represents three-fifths of the whole debt of the colony, and they bring in a net profit of £4 : 13 : 4 upon every hundred pounds. Together with the Customs, which their development tends largely to increase, they are estimated to yield this year £3,640,000 of the total revenue of £4,730,480, and in connection with their effect in increasing trade, and thereby adding to the Customs revenue, it may be interesting to note that the tonnage of vessels leaving and entering Cape ports has increased in the fifteen years since the construction of railways began in earnest to nearly seven times what it was before. The figures of the imports and exports for successive years are scarcely less satisfactory. The total for 1886, taken together, was £11,277,344. The total for last year, as given in the Treasurer's speech, exclusive of goods imported for the use of the Colonial and Imperial Governments, was £18,303,428. These figures have a double interest. They not only demonstrate the solid basis of the statement made by the Commissioner of Crown Lands in presenting his railway agreements to the House, to the effect that he has a good margin to come and go upon for working profit, and that if there is to be a war of rates between the Cape Colony and Natal it is not the Cape which will go to the wall, but they also show the very important place which the development of railways holds in the prosperity of the colony, and the security which they give to holders of colonial stock.

Assuming the position of the Natal railways to be relatively as good — and as to this I have no information beyond the published statement that they pay an interest of £4 : 12 : 7 per cent upon the invested capital of between three and four millions — it is still evident that in case of a commercial war, where the opposing hosts are represented by 16,000,000 on the one side and 4,000,000 on the other, the 16,000,000 are likely to win. In the trials of their strength both may, however, suffer considerably, and as they are neither of them private commercial enterprises, but Government undertakings — that is to say, really the property of the taxpayers of each colony — the public has not the selfish interest that it otherwise might have in seeing them ruin themselves for the consumers' benefit. Still less would it be economically sound that they should ruin themselves for the benefit of the Transvaal.

The proposal which this condition of things leads up to is that a railway union should be formed between the South African colonies and States, and the tariffs become a matter of mutual agreement. The Netherlands Railway Company is in everything but name the Transvaal Government. There is no reason, therefore, why this railway should not be included in the union. The differing interests of the uniting States would, it is contended, be a sufficient guarantee that rates would be kept down to a reasonably low figure, and they would be fixed in a fair proportion to working expenses, so that each Government would still have the incentive to good management which is at present supplied by open competition. The whole is simply a question of the distribution of taxes.

The result aimed at by the advocates of the railway union is to be able to maintain the present system of indirect taxation through the railway rates, which has been found to be a cheap and convenient form of collecting revenue. The argument of their opponents is that to use railway rates as a form of taxation is to undo with one hand what has been done by the other, and to stultify the development which the construction of railways is intended to promote. An excise tax and a tax on diamonds are both of them thrown in the teeth of the Cape Government when it argues the advantage of railway rates. Even to touch these questions is to show what a wide field of discussion the subject opens. As the matter stands at present it is believed that when existing sources of friction have been removed between the English Government and the Dutch Republic the Transvaal will be willing to enter the union. A provisional basis of rates has already been discussed and informally agreed to. The intentions of Natal are not known either at Bloemfontein or in Cape Town. It is presumable that if she is about to get responsible government the question will be left for a responsible Ministry to decide.

I had hoped, in writing from this place, to be able to enter also into the question of Customs Union, which hangs so closely upon railway development and is just now a matter of the keenest interest to the Free State. My letter is already so long that I must confine myself to indicating in the briefest possible manner how in this matter, as well as in the matter of railways, the Free State has within the last two or three years begun to make its influence felt in the South African Councils.

Having no port of its own, the Orange Free State has always been in the hands of its neighbours with regard to the Customs dues which they choose to levy upon goods passing through to its borders. In 1889 it entered, as I have mentioned, into a Customs Union with the Cape, and agreed to a common tariff of $12\frac{1}{2}$ *ad valorem*, or 17 per cent upon rateable articles. Of this sum it receives three-fourths, and one-fourth is kept by the Cape for transit dues. The arrangement has been on the whole extremely advantageous to the Orange Free State and has added something like a hundred thousand a year to its revenue. But Natal approves as little of the Cape Customs dues as of Cape railway rates. Goods pass through its ports at an average of from 5 to 7 per cent less than they pay at the Cape. The inhabitants of the north-eastern districts of the Free State, who are in the habit of drawing their supplies across the border from Natal, now find themselves obliged to pay the higher rate fixed by the Customs Union. They naturally object, and as they have a strong representation in the Volksraad of the Free State they are able to make their objections strongly felt.

The Free State is thus to some extent divided between itself, and the Government, unwilling to resign the advantage which it has already gained from its participation in the union, is anxious to see Natal join the bond and equalise the rates on the basis, perhaps, of a slightly lower tariff all round. In order to obtain this concession it might be willing to concede something to Natal in the matter of railway extension. Natal, however, has lately replied to the overtures made by the Free State that she is not disposed to enter, or even to meet in conference to discuss, any Customs Union which does not include the Transvaal. As her principal trade is with the Transvaal this decision is not to be wondered at, and the Government of the Free State is now endeavouring to use its influence in Pretoria to overcome the objections of President Kruger. The two Republics have an agreement of their own which amounts to free trade in local produce, but their trade relations would be greatly simplified by the extension of the union. The Free State has, therefore, everything to gain by drawing the Transvaal into the South African bond. Hence the interest taken here in the settlement of the Swazi question and the resolution passed not long ago by the Raad to make a representation upon the subject to the Imperial Government.

VI

MASERU, BASUTOLAND.

PERHAPS the prettiest part of the Free State is that which lies between Bloemfontein and the borders of Basutoland. No train at present crosses it, and in order to reach Maseru it is necessary in the first instance to drive to Ladybrand upon the Free State frontier. The distance is about 80 miles, and the post-cart, which leaves Bloemfontein at five in the morning, reaches Ladybrand at six in the evening. It is a canvas-tented vehicle on springs, drawn by eight horses, and is much lighter and, on the whole, more comfortable than the coaches of the Transvaal. The driver handles a whip like a salmon-rod with much dexterity, and keeps the eight horses in a perpetual hand gallop, of which the speed increases rather than slackens when a river has to be crossed, or any specially bad piece of road to be got over.

The incidental effect upon the passengers is to cause them to make many involuntary excursions into the roof of the wagon, and the pleasure of the drive depends not a little upon the amount of activity with which you are prepared to play the part of shuttlecock to the battledore of the seat. It is not an exercise for the nervous, and the most nimble may lay their account with being moderately bruised by the end of the day; but, with due allowance for this drawback, the experience, as a whole, is not disagreeable. You are not all the time in river-beds nor on bad pieces of road, nor even on pebbly veldt, where loose gravel flies into your eyes, and if you have the fortunate chance that I had to be alone with the mail bags, and to have the canvas sides of the wagon looped up all round, so as to give an unobstructed view of the country as you pass through, you may spend some very enjoyable hours.

We began our journey by starlight, but the sun rose over the veldt about two hours after we had left Bloemfontein, and by the time the light had fully spread we were already entering an undulating country where hill-tops began to wreathe the horizon. Within four hours of Bloemfontein the veldt took the aspect of a yellow land upon which a child's Noah's ark had been set out. Herds of cattle and horses and flocks of sheep, with here and there a quaint figure wrapped in a blanket watching them, were scattered thickly over the landscape. There were no trees, no hedges, no dividing lines of any kind except those made passingly by the shadows of the clouds. There were no villages in the European sense, but from time to time a slope was dotted with the round and melon-shaped huts of a native settlement. The herds were of great extent, and must have represented a very considerable amount of wealth, but if the country had been swept of its cattle nothing of the value of half-a-crown would have been left.

As we drove on we met with more evidence of cultivation. Farm lands and gardens began to take the place of the pasturage, and by two o'clock we were in a district where maize stalks were still standing and the upland edges waved with corn. It was a peculiarly lovely day, bright, cold, and breezy, with clouds drifting across a dazzling sky. The hill-tops, which caught every colour of the rainbow from pink and pearl to a blue that was almost black, seemed at last to girdle completely a spreading garden of gold and green. It was the grain district of the Orange Free State which was taken from the Basutos after their last war, and is still known without any scruple of delicacy by the name of the Conquered Territory.

Every hour which brought us nearer to Basutoland gave more picturesqueness to the landscape. Late in the afternoon the road began to wind sharply up and down hill, and sunset found us on a high ridge with a magnificent view of the Maluti range spread out before us. " There," said the driver, with a comprehensive sweep of the salmon rod, " there is Basutoland, and there, and there, and there. All the mountains are Basutoland."

The horizon was filled from edge to edge with mountain-tops. Some of the higher peaks were already tipped with snow, and rose white and sharp from the ghostly grays of the eastern twilight; towards the west others were glowing red and purple under the reflections of the sky. It is the Switzerland of South Africa, a country of rocks and waterfalls and fertile valleys, and it bears in extent the same proportion to the Switzerland of Europe that the Orange Free State bears to France. It has an area of 10,293 miles, of which the greater part is mountain. Some day when the farmers of Ladybrand get their grain line to Bloemfontein and the manner of approach is easier, it will probably become the happy hunting ground of tourists in search of health and picturesque scenery. At present it is simply the home of one of the most promising of the native races of the continent.

Its history is not altogether unworthy of the geographic parallel, for if Basutoland is our Switzerland, the Basutos may fairly claim to be the Swiss of South Africa. They have defended their mountain fastnesses again and again with success against troops superior to them in armament and military knowledge, but they are not naturally warlike; they are, on the contrary, a peaceful, hardy, and industrious people. They number at present about 218,000, and the resident Europeans, including teachers, missionaries, and Government officials, do not reach the total of 600.

It will be remembered that after the last war, which resulted in the disannexation of Basutoland from the Cape Colony, a majority of the Basuto chiefs willingly accepted the direct rule of the Imperial Government, and in the month of March 1884 Sir Marshall Clarke took up the position which he now holds of Resident Commissioner. In order to appreciate what he has done, it is necessary to recall briefly the situation with which he had to deal.

He found the local chiefs fighting between themselves. Those who had been in favour of the Cape colonial connection were hard pressed, and fearing to be driven for refuge into the Orange Free State. Others were rebelling against the authority of their own paramount chief Letsia; others, again, against the district chiefs whom Letsia had appointed. A section of the people led by Masupha openly rejected the authority of the Imperial Government, and declined to pay hut tax. Quarrels between herdsmen led frequently to the "eating up"—that is, the wholesale destruction or sweeping away—of the cattle of an offending village.

Stock thefts were common upon the borders of the Orange Free State, and gave rise to violations of the Free State territory. A chief whose territory had been annexed by the Orange Free State had taken refuge in Basutoland with the avowed intention of exciting the sympathy of the native chiefs and stirring up difficulties upon the frontier. Fear had been aroused in the Free State that the Basuto natives would unite in an attempt to repossess themselves by force of arms of the conquered territory, and commandoes were on foot. To add to the disquiet a rumour spread during the first months of the new administration that the troops which were being raised for Sir Charles Warren's expedition to Bechuanaland were really intended to be directed against Basutoland for the purpose of abolishing the power of the chiefs, and Maseru, the capital, and Mafeteng, another of the English stations, were in consequence watched by large armed detachments of natives.

Side by side with all this incitement to violence the drink traffic was flourishing. Natives were everywhere leaving their fields to flock to the numerous canteens, and the Resident Commissioner's first report reckons among the "great difficulties" of the situation the fact that "since the rebellion the majority of the chiefs have become habitual drunkards." It was a position which has repeated itself again and again in native communities. War had temporarily demoralised a whole people, and

Basutoland was on the verge of falling into a condition of anarchy and degradation which would have rendered it a source of danger and disturbance, not only to its immediate neighbours, but to South Africa. Surrounded as it is by native populations in Natal, Zululand, and the Transkei, it needed little more to become a leaven of disorder, of which the effect would have been injuriously felt from the Zambesi to the Cape.

Sir Marshall Clarke's achievement has been to avert this peril without the employment of force, and to bring Basutoland in the course of eight years from the position in which he found it to the position which it at present holds as a centre of loyalty and order among native populations, and a source of supply of food and labour to the neighbouring States. The output of grain, cattle, and native produce from Basutoland last year reached the value of £250,000, and passes were issued to between 50,000 and 60,000 natives who went to work in the mines of Kimberley and Johannesburg. The drink traffic has been entirely stopped. For five years there has been no fighting between the chiefs. The practice of "eating up" cattle has been suppressed. Fair trial has been substituted for the arbitrary and barbarous custom of "smelling out," or, in other words, of torturing for witchcraft. Border disputes with the Orange Free State have been arranged, the frontier has been defined by a commission appointed for the purpose, and a large portion of it has been fenced. Roads are being made throughout Basutoland. Trading licences have increased in number. Industrial and other schools are spreading, and free dispensaries and cottage hospitals, which were at first regarded with distrust and dislike, have come into general use among the natives.

In 1891 Basutoland entered the Customs Union. This year it was connected by telegraph with the Orange Free State. In other words, peace has been substituted for war, and the customs of civilisation are daily gaining ground. From a source of danger the country has become a source of strength, and the most satisfactory feature of the whole situation is that the reforms which have been effected have been carried out always with the concurrence and in many cases through the agency of the chiefs.

I do not want to seem passingly to say that Basutoland may never again become a source of trouble or disturbance. Opinions differ too much upon the subject of the apparent loyalty of the actual chiefs, and native politics are too much complicated by distant issues for any such prophecy to be made. I only want, as far as it is possible in the very short limits of a letter, to indicate what has been done and the manner in which it has been done. It is not often that a man sees his work produce fruit under his hand as Sir Marshall Clarke has done, and the seven very short annual reports in which he catalogues the principal events of his administration form, taken together, one of the most interesting and instructive of the minor chapters of English history.

The system upon which he has worked rejects alike the theory that treats the native as a child irresponsible for his acts and dispossessed of personal rights and the theory which accepts him as a man and a brother equal in all things to his white neighbour. It deals with him as a man fully responsible for his acts, behind the white man in civilisation, but subject to precisely the same laws of human development, and it is based upon the principle that to develop his self-respect and to make him a useful member of society are almost synonymous terms. It is the principle upon which the best educational institutions for natives within the colony have accomplished all their admirable work, and the mission schools in Basutoland have contributed not a little to the success of the political experiment.

The most important of these are, curiously enough, not English. The French Protestant mission of the Paris Evangelical Society, which has for many years devoted its labours to the education of the Basuto people, has 13 principal stations and 129 out-stations, with day schools scattered through the country. It has nearly 8000 children upon its ordinary school rolls, and has, besides these, about 700 young men in training either as teachers or in industrial institutions where trades are taught.

At the principal station at Morija, which lies within a four hours' drive of Maseru, and within half an hour of the mountain kraal of Lerothodi, the present paramount chief, there is a printing and bookbinding establishment, where, on the occasion of my visit, an edition of 3000 copies of a Sesuto reading-book was under preparation entirely by native printers and compositors. A fortnightly paper, of which the name, being translated, means *The Little Light*, is also printed and published here in Sesuto. It is written principally by native contributors, and, far from experiencing any difficulty in keeping it alive, the editor has to complain of plethora of copy and want of space. It reaches, I learned, the very respectable circulation of 800 copies. The Government printing is also done by natives at Morija.

At Quthing, another of the English stations, there is an industrial school, where stone-cutting, masons' work, and carpentering are taught. At Thaba Bosigo, the historic burying-place of the chiefs, there is a school for girls, where, in addition to elementary education, the pupils can learn needlework, cookery, and the ordinary domestic arts. There are also excellent industrial schools for boys and girls supported by the French Roman Catholic mission at Roma, and there are some schools supported by the English Church. The value of them all is that, whatever their system of teaching, they are centres of civilisation, and achieve perhaps as much by the unconscious influence as by deliberate effort.

Every mission station that I visited had houses built of brick and well-planted gardens. Each had its church and schoolhouse, and it was noticeable that the huts which surrounded them were of distinctly higher grade than the huts of a purely native settlement. At Morija many were square, and possessed of the luxury of windows and an upright door. Some had chimneys. Three or four that I entered had European furniture. One was quite pretty, with blue-washed walls, chintz curtains, and blue willow-patterned cups and dishes on a shelf.

The step from an ordinary native hut to this is very great, and represents an advance in development of which the significance can hardly be exaggerated. It means nothing less than the conversion of the native from the condition of loafing savage to the condition of a labourer. This, if it could become general, is the solution of the native problem, and it is difficult to realise anywhere but on the spot how much the missionaries contribute to make it general. It is only, perhaps, in driving about the mountains, visiting alternately chiefs and mission stations, that it is possible to appreciate the real and best work that they are doing. By inducing the common people to adopt civilised customs, they are giving them civilised wants and laying the foundation of all civilised endeavour.

The great obstacle to the material development of South Africa is everywhere declared to be the scarcity of labour. With labour enough I was repeatedly told in the Transvaal we could do anything. The question of questions is how to obtain it. Here in the remote valleys of Basutoland, cultivated as they are from edge to edge, an answer seems dimly possible. Here a native population is at work. Before long the difficulty will be that no more land will remain to be taken up. Still the population is increasing, and every year sends out larger numbers to earn money beyond the borders. Basutoland under orderly administration is becoming a labour reserve. Why should not this be the case with all native territories? They are looked upon at present as the cloud upon the South African horizon. If they could by any means be converted into communities of labourers, they would become, on the contrary, the natural pendant in South African prosperity of the immense wealth which is waiting to be developed.

There are, of course, great difficulties in the way.

A question which has perplexed successive generations and given rise to so many bitter struggles is not likely to settle itself hurriedly now merely because its settlement becomes every day more urgent. Yet there are certain conclusions that may, I think, be fairly drawn from conditions which exist now and have never existed in South Africa before. The first of these is that the native question and the labour question are rapidly merging themselves in one, and are consequently engaging the attention of two very different classes of minds. Men who have never worked together before are likely to be found in the future in cordial co-operation and to lend to each other's schemes all the weight of combined conviction. In coming from the Transvaal to Basutoland this impression is most striking.

For all practical purposes there are but two questions which are of any real importance in the South Africa of to-day. One is the material development; the other is the race question. Everything which appears on the political field falls under one heading or the other, and it may be taken as a fair test of the value of any given measure how much it helps the one without hindering the other.

Generally speaking, the problems of material development enlist in their solution a different class of energy from that which lends itself willingly to the more abstract questions of race. In the Transvaal the first, in Basutoland the second may be seen in its typical expression, and both are at this moment working towards exactly the same result. The men who are most eagerly occupied in making their own fortunes in Johannesburg are strongly of opinion that, somehow or other, the native must be made to work. If wages are the means by which he can be tempted, they are willing to pay him well. They do not care in the least about him; they care only for the profit which they foresee for themselves from the result, and within the limits which leave a dividend he is welcome to what he wants. Their only source of annoyance is that they cannot get as many workmen as they want, and, if it would advance matters, they would probably be ready to pay a premium to every missionary, official, or philanthropist who turned a labourer into the market.

In Basutoland, for absolutely different reasons, the object of all endeavour is the same. Here it is felt that the true place of the native in the South African community for generations to come will be the place of a labourer. There is no finality in politics, and there is no desire to limit his future possibilities, but it is evident, in the opinion of his best friends, that in his uneducated condition he has not reached the average level of the labourer. He must take the first step before he can be prepared for those that follow, and industry must for a long time to come be his religion. Here education is doing what compulsory labour Bills have not yet been found competent to effect, and a generation of natives is growing up with requirements which can only be satisfied by working.

As a labourer the native takes at once a new place in the social scale. He is an element in the development of the country. He becomes valuable and will be valued accordingly. Seeing then that he has himself everything to gain by filling the place which the conditions of the country open to him, that the need for his services will only increase as the material development of the north goes on, and that the labour question is the next great question which is likely to engage the attention of South African politicians of all schools, it does not seem too much to hope that what is happening in the Transvaal and Basutoland may be a type and forerunner of what will take place throughout South Africa.

VII

KING WILLIAM'S TOWN.

BY whatever route you determine to descend from the High Veldt of the interior to the southern coast, you no sooner leave the crest of the high ground behind you than you become aware of the softening influence of the airs from the Indian Ocean. I came down from De Aar Junction, which is the meeting-point of the Eastern, Western, and Midland railway system of the colony, to Port Elizabeth, and from Port Elizabeth by sea to East London. The descent is made in five great steps, through wild, but no longer treeless, scenery. Mountain passes, covered with euphorbias, flowering aloes, and aromatic herbage, alternate in succession with plateaux that widen out to farm and pasture lands. In places the rocky sides are aflame with scarlet blossom, then there come long stretches of grass as green as the meadows of Essex, and the low scrub and bush of ostrich farms. There is no fine timber, but all the edges of the hills are wooded, the hollows are full of flowers. Throughout the day the northern horizon is boldly outlined by the hills we have descended, and to the south ever widening valleys open towards blue distances that represent the sea.

We left De Aar at two in the morning with a

sharp frost that made us glad to cower round the fire in the waiting-room and warm our hands and feet before the train started. By sunset we are on a warm level where ostrich farms have become frequent, and the long-legged birds, disturbed by the whistle of the train, race the engine and outstrip our speed with apparently little effort. In the dark we cross the Addo veldt, where elephants still roam in a wild state. Port Elizabeth is represented only by a semicircle of harbour lights round an uncomfortably rough sea, and it is afternoon again before a tug is steaming with us up the Buffalo River to East London. Three more hours of climbing in the train take us up to the 1700 feet level upon which King William's Town stands.

These long and rapid journeys serve to bring the continent and its varying capacities and conditions together with a curiously kaleidoscopic effect. When you begin to count the miles you have traversed by thousands, you feel that you have at least seen something of the physical surface and shape of a country in which a mere handful of Europeans are laying the foundations of future history, and just as in the turning of a kaleidoscope there are certain blue and red spots which always attract the eye and form the centre of each new combination, so in this great extent of physical surface which you are every day looking at from some new point of view there are certain constant elements which form the centre of every conceivable combination of its historical development. The blue and red spots of the South African kaleidoscope, which may change in their relation to each other and in the effect which they produce upon the whole, but which must remain permanently as the component parts of its design, are the immense wealth and size of the country and the various forms of humanity which have met within its borders. The question of material development and the question of race are the two interests round which everything else revolves.

In the Transvaal, at Kimberley, in the Northern territory of the Chartered Company, in Bechuanaland, in Natal, ever since the advent of the railway in the Free State, material is the subject of daily talk and daily effort. The opening of means of communication, the development of mines, the settlement of land are matters of vital and of always increasing importance. They form the aim of all practical political politics. But this constructive work is being carried on over an area of millions of square miles by the initiative of little more than half a million of persons.

The entire white population of South Africa, including the Dutch Republics, amounts to only 620,000. The task that they have undertaken is nothing less than Titanic, and it is evident that whatever may be the mental energy, however inexhaustible the stock of initiative that may have prompted its conception, actual motive power is still deficient. South Africa cannot be ploughed from the Zambesi to the Cape, nor its cities built, nor its rivers bridged by half a million of hands. Manual labour, and manual labour in large quantities, is absolutely essential to success. Labour is, therefore, rapidly becoming the supreme demand of the white population.

But the white population is not the only population of South Africa. Side by side with this amount of material development, which seems to determine the future of the white race, there is also the question of the future of the black race. A complete census of natives cannot, of course, be taken. But their numbers are to be certainly counted by millions. Within the Cape Colony and Natal alone they reach nearly 2,000,000. Throughout the still independent or partially protected native territories they swarm uncounted, and there are many districts in which the future of these wild races and their relation to the South Africa of coming history is the all-absorbing topic of thought. Basutoland is one of those districts. King William's Town, situated as it is in the very heart of a native population, upon the borders of the Transkei, where nearly half a million of natives still live under the rule of their tribal chiefs, and within a day's journey of barbaric Pondoland, where the ruling chief, Sigcan, roasted his stepmother the other day, and habitually fastens offenders against his sovereign pleasure into ant-heaps to be eaten alive, is another.

Here the hum and bustle of material development sounds faintly from the far distant levels of the High Veldt, and the native question is all important. And as in the Transvaal, as in Basutoland, so here the outcome of all serious thought upon the subject appears to be the conclusion that the two great problems of South Africa ought to solve each other, that the difficulty which hampers the question of material development and the difficulty which stands in the way of the satisfactory progress of the native races are in truth one and the same, that both would be removed and the successful future of South Africa assured if any system or process could be devised by which the average raw native could be converted into an effective labourer.

Already, as I have said, in Basutoland the desire to convert the native into a labourer is uniting the endeavours of the missionaries and the officers charged with the duties of administration. The chiefs have been induced to appreciate the solid advantages which result both to themselves and to their people, and the effect has been eminently satisfactory. Not only is the whole Basuto nation at work within its own frontiers, but as the land is more and more taken up it sends increasing numbers of labourers out to the mining centres in which labour is in demand. Fifty or sixty thousand, which is the number of passes granted every year to natives going across the frontier to work, is not a bad percentage upon a population of 217,000.

When the position of which Basutoland offers at present only a small practical illustration can be repeated in some of its essential particulars throughout South Africa, and philanthropists, practical politicians, and native leaders unite heartily in the endeavour to induce the native masses to become labouring masses, it can be scarcely doubtful that some sort of similar success will be achieved. There are signs that this condition of things is by the force of circumstances likely to be brought about. The hard-and-fast line which used to exist between the missionary and the politician, the negrophobist, and the practical business man, is disappearing. It is becoming apparent that the same object may legitimately enlist all their efforts.

The composition of the present Government of

the Cape, including, as it does, men of the negrophobist traditions of Mr. Rose Innes and Mr. Sauer and a number of the Africander Bond, with such moving spirits of material development as Mr. Rhodes and Mr. Sivewright, is something more than an accident. It is almost an inevitable outcome of the convergence of public thought. It is certainly typical of the various sides from which the next great question with which the country will be called upon to deal may be approached. There is little doubt that this question is the labour question. The passing of the franchise measure has prepared the way for it; the still more difficult question of liquor remains to be dealt with. Behind them both lies the object which some people think cannot be touched by legislation—namely, the distribution of native labour through those parts of the colony or the continent in which it is most required.

At present about four-fifths of the native population of the colony are collected in the eastern district and the native territories which neighbour upon it. The Fingoes number about a quarter of a million. The Transkei and the territories of Griqualand East, Tembuland, etc., contain about another half-million. Basutoland has not far from a quarter of a million. The district of King William's Town alone contains more than 70,000 natives. Deduct all these from the million and a quarter which the census gave to the whole colony, and it will be seen in how large a proportion they cluster round this neighbourhood. It is not that in this part of the colony there is most work for them to do. Quite the contrary. The industrial and agricultural centres are at Kimberley and in the Western district. But here are their locations and reserves. There, if they wish to live, they must work. Here, the incentive to work has been taken from them. Food and shelter in perpetuity have been assured to them.

In the territories which have been annexed since 1875 there is a total area of something like 14,000 square miles, which in its moral effect upon the native population may be compared to a gigantic pauper asylum. Within the limits of a location or reserve no native who has a wife need work, nor need he fear to starve. The principle of the location is that the land is owned by the community and is inalienable. It is cultivated by the women, and the man who owns women has consequently a provision of land and labour of which he cannot be deprived. It is entirely unaffected by his own conduct, and the principle of individual responsibility, upon which the framework of civilised society rests, is non-existent. The ordinary equipment of the raw Kaffir is a blanket, which he brings to a very picturesque tint of terra-cotta by braying it with powdered red ochre. He may add a few blue and white beads by way of decoration, but he needs no further wearing apparel nor sleeping accommodation. Wrapped in his blanket, he is to be seen sitting in the sun in all the locations of the Eastern district. His wives sow and reap and grind and cook the maize upon which he lives. He has not learned to care for luxuries, his necessaries are all provided. Why, in the name of common sense, he may well ask, should he work? We have heard a great deal at home about the pauperisation of the working classes. Curiously, it does not yet seem to have been realised by the friends of the native on what a vast scale it has been practised here.

The well-intentioned philanthropy which has assured to every individual native an inalienable share in the property of his tribe has, it is true, saved South Africa from the existence of a class whose material wants are unprovided for, but it has done so at the cost of the permanent degradation of the native race. All impulse to personal effort has been removed. The situation which has been created is entirely artificial, for, in a savage state, the man was obliged to defend by force the possessions in which the stronger powers of civilisation now maintain him. While his women worked he fought, and, if the conditions of his existence were not ideal, they called at least for natural exertion. In his actual condition he is an excrescence upon creation, useful to no one, and least of all to himself. His friends still endeavour to repair with one hand what has been destroyed with the other. Having deprived him of the initial incentive which is embodied in our own harsh, wholesome doctrine that the man who does not work shall not eat, they hope to coax him into the way he should go by inspiring him with more complicated needs.

The difficulty, it is often said, is that the native has no wants. If we could give him wants he would work to satisfy them. This is the object of the most enlightened missionary efforts, and to some extent it has been successfully attained. A class of native who is distinguished from his less enlightened brethren by the title of School Kaffir has been brought into existence. The School Kaffir can read and write, can wear European dress, and acquires a taste for European habits which leads him in many instances to work. Domestic servants and labourers come largely from this class, and it forms an element which, in spite of many faults and the general disrepute which is sure to attend an artificially educated section of any people, is not to be despised. But at present the School Kaffir is a creature apart, and it happens often enough that the distance which has been placed by education between him and his fellows is too great to be maintained, and by a not unnatural reaction he falls back entirely to the level from which he started. Some people attribute this to a misdirection of educating effort, and are of opinion that the endeavour to make a skilled native artisan is as much out of place as the endeavour to make learned native professors.

There is no general demand in the colony nor among the natives themselves for artisans. All that is wanted and that will be wanted for a long time to come is labourers, grooms, gardeners, ploughmen, miners, porters, men willing to use their muscles and submit to the discipline of daily exertion. Anything finer than this, it is urged, will not be wanted and will not be paid for. Consequently, it will fall under the practically inoperative head of the disused accomplishment. An instance in point falls under my eyes here, in the person of a native who holds a position in the service of the Woods and Forests. He was educated at Lowedale, and is, I am told, an accomplished cabinetmaker. He has a hut and a bit of ground out in the bush. He wears a blanket, has two or three wives, and to the best belief of his superior officer never does a day's work from year's end to year's end. Nobody in his world wanted cabinets, he did not care for them himself, and he prefers to draw pay for the labour of his wives. I mention the case because it has a typical value.

If it were possible by education to instil a taste for luxuries into a people already possessed of the necessaries of life, the work of refining and developing the race would only be a question of time. But, when we take into account the frequent lapses of this kind which occur, it seems to be a matter of grave doubt whether the best meant efforts can do more than touch the fringe of the whole matter, as long as the first inward spur to action which rests upon the hard groundwork of necessity is absent. This view is further supported by the fact that, when for any reason crops fail and supplies in the locations become scanty, labour becomes at once plentiful in the surrounding neighbourhood. It is only employers who live in a district surrounded on all sides by locations that are able to note the immediate fluctuations of the labour barometer.

In times of plenty in the locations a cook may not be scolded, a groom may not be kept out at night, a gardener may not be asked to cut an extra supply of vegetables, without fear of finding that the domestic in question prefers a return to the location to further service. In times of scarcity good manners and attentive performance of duties may be expected. But, though the effect of the condition of the location upon the supply of labour is more immediately noticed here, it none the less makes itself felt throughout South Africa, and it is now coming to be generally admitted that the existence of the location is the primary cause of the deficiency in the supply of native labour.

There are, however, some other recognised causes which it is well not to lose sight of. Among these is the not altogether surprising fact that, while many would-be employers complain of being unable to obtain labour, their real trouble is not that they cannot get labour but that they cannot get it at their own price.

Farmers want a compulsory labour law in order that they may be sure of a cheap as well as of a plentiful labour supply. The wages which they offer in this neighbourhood vary from 5s. to 15s. a month with food, and this is not enough. Natives will not leave the location to take it. It is vain to say that the amount of wages makes no difference, that the native is inherently lazy and that nothing but force will compel him to work. Force is a very different thing from natural necessity, and the difference between the operation of the one and the other is all the difference between a race of workmen and a race of slaves. Failing necessity, superior inducement is the only resource, and that this will act even under present conditions is demonstrated by the evidence of Kimberley, Johannesburg, and Basutoland. In all these places the native has shown not only that he can work, but that he will work, if for any reason it becomes worth his while. Up to this point there is not one of us who is not essentially lazy.

The native only follows a human law, and it cannot be too soon or too clearly recognised that any hopes of obtaining labour from him at a price lower than that which he chooses to set upon it are hopes which mean nothing less than slavery in disguise, and are foredoomed to disappointment. To endeavour to compel him to work by means of an increased taxation is also a mere tinkering at the question, which is not likely to produce much impression. Fair wages, which, as long as he works only for luxuries, will necessarily be high wages—and, it is regrettable to be obliged to add, faithful observance of the terms of agreement—combined, perhaps, with some modification of the existing Masters and Servants Act, appear to represent the best that can be done while the present system of locations and tribal tenure of land remains in force.

The experience of Kimberley, Johannesburg, Basutoland, Khama's country, and Natal—in fact all experience of any value—would add to these a preventive liquor law. But when all this has been done the fundamental question will still remain to be faced. Is it necessary, or wise, or right to continue a system of land tenure which puts natives outside the operation of the natural impulse to work for a living, and deprives them at the same time of the dignified sense of individual responsibility? The difficulties in the way of abolishing such a system are, of course, many and great. How they could best be met must be a question for experts. The fairer principle would seem to be to proceed by some gradual system of survey and allotment into individual freehold.

The idea that the native cannot understand the system of freehold is exploded by the experience of Natal, where natives are becoming in increasing quantities freeholders of land purchased from the Crown. In Natal it is held that the practice of monogamy follows the plough—that is to say, that a more enlightened system of agriculture has a tendency to do away with the plurality of wives, who, under the old system, represent little more than farm labourers. However this may be, there is no doubt that the issue of individual title in the locations, if such a thing were by any means feasible, would greatly facilitate the advance of civilisation and the abolition of old and savage customs, among which polygamy ranks, perhaps, as one of the least harmful. Unquestionably one result of the issue of individual title would be that many natives would part with their land. This would be far from an unmixed evil. In the first place, those who did so would be henceforth dependent upon their own exertions, and consequently of necessity labourers. In the second place, the mass of the native locations would be by degrees broken up, and the million or so of natives who now congregate in this part of South Africa would be little by little distributed throughout the colonies and States, and thus become more easily absorbed in the natural channels of labour and civilisation.

The probable tendency of such a distribution would be towards the centres of material development where they are needed. Thus, while competition lessened the price of labour, a larger number of labourers would be employed, and the material basis of South African prosperity might be laid by native hands, for the mutual benefit and advancement of black and white races alike. Liquor and land, it has been truly said, constitute the two great elements of the native question. Add labour to these, and it must be admitted that the result is a trinity of the most difficult subjects with which modern legislation is called upon to deal. When they have been dealt with here, the South African race question will have disappeared, and it is not the least interesting part of the in many respects unique problem which it presents, that it should thus involve a settlement under its own conditions of the same questions which are perplexing all the world.

VIII

PIETERMARITZBURG, NATAL.

THE coast journey from East London to Natal is generally rough enough for bad sailors to be glad to salve their pride with the, I imagine, seldom varying assurance that the trip is one of the very worst which falls within the long experience of the captain; but it has the advantage of being all the time within sight of land, so that while the hours of daylight last there is at least the diversion of studying the shore.

Pondoland, with its hills and woods and waterfalls, takes up the greater part of a day. There is scarcely a harbour along the inhospitable line into which even a small boat can enter. The rivers flow from the mountains of the interior across ground which is still high when it reaches the sea, and they fall over the cliff's edge in waterfalls that in the rainy season become magnificent. Only a few have already cut their channels down into gorges through the rock. Among these is the St. John's, which is navigable for vessels of small draught at the mouth, and of which the gates, as they are called, form the picturesque show spot of the coast. They are simply the two sides of a table-mountain, over the edge of which the river may once have fallen, as the smaller rivers still fall on either hand. It is now cleft from the summit to the base, and the river flows out naturally through a wooded valley to the sea-level. It is a little port of civilisation which was annexed by the Cape Government, it may be remembered, about eight years ago. But for it and the eight-mile strip on either bank of the river which belongs to it, the barbarism of Pondoland is unbroken. Over the three or four thousand square miles of territory of which it is composed, the rule of the savage is still supreme.

The stories of cruelty perpetrated by command of the chiefs, which are from time to time carried over the border, are sickening in their atrocity, and you wonder, as your glass sweeps the shore, what scenes of horror its beauty hides. Lying, as Pondoland does, like a wedge of savagery between the civilised borders of the Cape Colony and Natal, its annexation can be merely a question of time; and as Natal has already a sufficiently extensive native area to occupy her energies in Zululand, it is more than probable that the Cape Colony will before long deal with the question. The sooner it does so the better, will be the general opinion.

If it incorporates Pondoland absolutely with its own territory, its frontier will then be conterminous with the frontier of Natal; and the reasons which are strong already for the friendly co-operation of the two English colonies in the settlement of South African questions will be by so much the stronger. That they ought to co-operate is one of the self-evident facts which the more liberal-minded public men of both colonies do not dispute. At the same time, it is unfortunately no less evident that on every question of South African interest with which both are concerned they stand at present opposed. It is difficult for the smaller colony to pardon the exercise of strength and energy by which the Cape has, as it were, stretched its limbs across the peninsula, and laid hands upon the Transvaal trade.

Natal is before all things a trading community, and the trade of the Transvaal and a portion of the Free State seemed only a few years ago to be hers of right for ever. Now it is flowing from her down the easy channel of the Cape and Free State Railway, and when she is invited to enter into a railway union it is not unnatural that she should feel a little sore at being asked to divide profits which she had speculated upon as all her own. The bitter part of the position is that, however pluckily she may compete, she has no choice. The most logical exposition of her natural rights goes down before the still harder logic of facts. The Cape Railway is in Johannesburg, or will be before many weeks have passed, whereas the Natal extension is still stationary on the Transvaal border, waiting for permission to come on. Every week that passes makes the position worse, for the habit of trading through Port Elizabeth gains ground. The authorities of Natal agree with the authorities of the Cape on the general theory that to come to an understanding with each other and fix a tariff which will enable both railway systems to run at a profit is better than to continue a cut-throat competition which must injure both, even though it should stop short of ruining one. The difficulty in the present sore state of feeling is to fix upon a practical basis for the tariff. The mileage of the

Natal lines to Johannesburg and Pretoria, supposing them finished, would be so much less than the mileage of the Cape lines that, if the charge for the carriage of goods were fixed on a basis of so much per mile, Natal would have an immense advantage over the Cape. She claims for herself that she has a right to this advantage, which comes from her geographical position.

The Cape, on the other hand, contends that what is gained geographically is lost topographically, and that the expense of construction and working upon a line of which the ruling gradient is 1 in 30 is so great that, if the two railway systems were run on strictly commercial principles, it would be found that the Cape line could afford to carry goods at a lower rate from point to point than the Natal line could do. The desire of the Cape is, therefore, for a tariff fixed on a point-to-point basis. But if the point-to-point charge were equal, Natal trade would be altogether ruined, for the greater nearness of the Cape ports to Europe and America would give an advantage to the Cape against which there would be no competition.

Natal cannot evidently accept an arrangement which means ruin to herself. The union tariff, if there is one, must be fixed on a compromise between these two extremes. Natal must have some allowance made for her natural advantage in having about 200 miles less of road to run; the Cape must have some allowance for the geographical position of her ports and the topographical advantages of her railway road. What this allowance should be on either side must be a matter of discussion. It has been suggested to pool the railways and divide the profits. This might be satisfactory from the point of view of the Governments concerned, but it would not satisfy the local demands of the various ports, nor simplify the discussion of interests to any appreciable extent.

The difficulty in approaching the discussion would be less if the two colonies were in other respects in an equal position; but here again the facts are merciless. The Cape is the premier State of South Africa. It is larger, stronger, richer, and more populous than Natal. Its resources are more varied, and it gains every day the increased impetus in development which comes of successful progress. It is useless to endeavour to escape from the inevitable, and the wise policy for the smaller colony would seem to be to acknowledge in a loyal and friendly spirit the supremacy which cannot be denied. But Natal is unable to accept this position.

The feeling here is that the Cape misuses its strength for the purpose of crushing and oppressing its weaker neighbours, and that the only hope of obtaining a fair bargain is to be in a position to extort it. There is, consequently, a much greater inclination towards alliance with the Republics against the dominant power than there is towards alliance with the other English colony, and, with the hope before it of obtaining advantageous concessions from the Transvaal, Natal is not disposed at present to discuss the question of Railway Union on amicable terms. There is a confident belief that the survey which has been voted by the Volksraad for the extention of the Natal line from Charlestown will very shortly be followed by the construction of the line, and it is held that when this is done Natal will be able to treat on a more equal footing as regards railway matters with the Cape.

It is needless to say that the Transvaal draws its own advantage from the situation and is not anxious to contribute in any way to the soothing of colonial susceptibilities. The position with regard to Customs Union has much the same admixture of fact and feeling. The Cape and Free State have entered into a Customs Union, which is without doubt very advantageous to the Free State. The Free State, having no port of its own, was dependent, before it entered into the Customs Union, upon the tariff of its neighbours. If the Cape imposed a duty of 12 per cent, goods which came through Cape ports paid 12 per cent. If the duty of Natal was 5 per cent, goods which came through the ports of Natal paid 5 per cent. In neither case did the Government of the Free State receive anything, and it was natural that the importer who had to pay the dues preferred goods which came by way of Natal. Natal had fair reason to look upon the Free State trade as an increasing quantity in her future. But here again the Cape stepped in and narrowed the field. By the agreement of the Customs Union the Free State accepts the duties of the Cape, imposes them upon all its borders, and receives in return a three-quarters share from the Cape Customs of all the duties levied on Free State goods. This amounts, in round numbers, to about £100,000 a year. Natal goods going up pay first their own duty at the port, then the Customs Union duty on the frontier. Instead of benefit, they suffer considerable disadvantage, and, as with the Transvaal, so with the Free State, force of circumstances is driving Natal trade to the Cape.

Again the Cape offers an agreement. Enter, it says, into our Customs Union, and again Natal refuses to act under compulsion. The average Customs dues collected within the Union, taking rateable and *ad valorem* articles together, is found to be about 17 per cent. The same average taken for Natal gives 8 per cent. To enter the Customs Union at present would mean for Natal something slightly more than doubling its present duties. In addition to this, Natal politicians object to the principle of, as they express it, taxing bread and letting brandy go free. If they consented to enter a Customs Union at all, it would be on condition that the average duty was lowered, and that necessaries of life should be, as far as possible, untaxed. At present, moreover, the condition of inter-colonial free trade, which accompanies Customs Union, is of comparatively little value to Natal, for the freedom is to obtain only over conterminous land frontiers and will not apply to colonial goods carried by sea.

The principal product which Natal has to offer to South Africa is sugar. If it enters a Cape port by sea it can do so only on the same terms as the sugar of Mauritius. To send it overland is too expensive. Tea, again, if it goes by sea, competes with Ceylon and must have no better terms. Briefly, as matters stand, Natal would, in its own opinion, suffer the disadvantages of Customs Union, and gain no corresponding benefit. It is not yet strong enough, it thinks, to enter the Union with the prospect of exerting sufficient influence to modify the conditions to which it objects, and it prefers to strengthen its hand in its own way by co-operation with the Transvaal. It has lost its advantage in the Free State trade because the Free State has entered the Union, but the Transvaal has not entered the Union, and until it does Natal hopes to keep a certain advantage in the Transvaal. The advantage is not very great, for the Cape gives a rebate to Transvaal goods in bond, which brings their duty down to the Natal rate. The difference applies chiefly to the sorted-up trade. This in the nature of things cannot benefit by rebate, and a great deal is at present done with Natal, bringing perhaps other trade in its train.

The danger of the situation is apparent. Natal stands in isolation from the Cape and Free State and trusts to the friendship of the Northern Republic. But President Kruger is bound to consider his own interests, and the day which sees some exciting causes of friction removed between him and the larger colony is not unlikely to see him also frankly espouse the views of the Cape in relation to South African politics. He may find himself constrained to abandon his present attitude of coquetting with Natal. He may refuse to encourage the extension of the railway from Charlestown. He may, as he is pledged to do in the event of the Transvaal's obtaining Swaziland and a port, bring the Republic into the Customs Union, in which case Natal would stand entirely alone. Or, as his own new tariff suggests, he may put so fierce a protective barrier round his borders as to drive all external trade to the same distance. In any of these events the position of Natal becomes extremely precarious. It is impossible that she should ignore the peril, and it is with a view to steadying her foothold and carrying her safely through any crisis which may be before her, that the more active spirits among her public men are desirous of obtaining for her all the liberties and the power of responsible government. They think she has been hampered in her dealings with the neighbouring States by the inequality of her position. The neighbouring States are self-governing; she is not. They are responsible for their actions; she is in tutelage still. In difficult circumstances it may happen that Natal, small as she is, is under the government of a minority, and the other South African Governments, knowing that her public men are unable to enforce the expression of their views, treat them with a disdain which is humiliating.

These circumstances have, it is thought, paralysed her action and weakened her decisions at critical moments, and the men who have developed her trade and built her railways and created her towns claim for themselves that they are as well able to take the management of political as of municipal affairs. They contend that they know their own interests, and can conduct their own negotiations concerning them better than any paternal Government. More than this, they claim that if mistakes are made they will suffer more willingly for mistakes of which they have the full responsibility than they can suffer for the mistakes of other people. In other words, they feel themselves to be fully grown, and the state of prolonged childhood is increasingly irksome. The colony refuses to deal with each individual point now under discussion until it holds a stronger position with regard to each. The desire for responsible government springs from a belief that in obtaining it the whole colonial position will be strengthened from root to branch.

Against this view there are many and not trifling objections. In the first place, there is, of course, the native question. The natives of Natal are numerically as ten to one of the white population. To ask for entire control of this immense mass is to ask for something which affects the well-being not only of Natal, but of all South Africa. It is not, therefore, to be wondered at that the Imperial Government should have thought it desirable to reserve the control of native affairs in its own hands. That it has done so has nevertheless weakened the chance of responsible government being carried at the elections by that substantial majority which is required. There are many advocates of the change, especially among the up-country Dutch voters, who are not inclined to consider that half a loaf is better than no bread, and who will reject it if hampered by this condition. They hardly give weight enough to the fact that if, as would undoubtedly be the case, the Imperial Government would have to bear the brunt of any trouble arising out of native mismanagement it is but just that it should keep a preponderating voice in the management; and, without considering that they have not so far had much to complain of in the Imperial administration of that section of their affairs, they join their voices to those of other opponents of the change, who, looking at the matter from an exactly opposite point of view, fear the withdrawal of the Imperial troops.

There can be no question that a colony which desires the comparative independence of responsible government must be prepared to provide for the maintenance of order within its own borders. If it cannot do this, the responsibility which it proposes to assume is simply the right to act as it pleases at some one else's expense. Without touching the question of external defence, there are men who think that the peace and order which at present distinguish the native population would not be maintained without the symbol of authority which is embodied in the red coat and the musket. They do not anticipate that the musket will be ever used, but they think that its presence is required. Men who hold this view will not accept a scheme of responsible government which makes no definite provision for the continuance of an Imperial garrison in the colony. Others, from a less worthy motive, object to see the troops withdrawn because their presence means the outlay of a certain amount of money.

The vote of Pietermaritzburg, where the troop money is mainly spent, will, it is supposed, be almost unanimously given against the change. Durban will, on the contrary, vote with equal unanimity in favour of it. Besides the counterbalancing fears with regard to native questions and the troops, there is the doubt, always felt in small communities, of whether there are a sufficient number of men free to give their energies to politics to form both a Ministry and an Opposition. The position of Natal, which is so far from lying absolutely smooth before her, is one in which careless or inefficient administration of her finances might bring about serious disaster, and in the party which is opposed to responsible government there exists some grave apprehension on this head. At Durban, however, I found business men, who would,

I imagine, be among the first to suffer in such a contingency, very confident that there was no ground for the fear. In their view, the introduction of responsible government will bring the best men in the colony into politics, and they see no reason to doubt that the same ability which has built up the trade of Natal will know how to protect the situation which has been created.

Apart from the native question, the interests of Natal are entirely commercial and agricultural, and when her merchants point to Durban and its surroundings and claim that, having created and organised these, they have proved themselves capable of administering their own affairs, it is impossible to deny that they have some justification.

The struggle for responsible government will be closely fought. Its most sincere supporters are not confident of the issue, for they recognise the weight of some of the practical objections which are urged against it. They believe that if they win they will greatly strengthen the position of Natal among South African States, and this is a result which, no matter how it is brought about, may be honestly welcomed on all sides.

The rivalry which exists at present between the two English colonies is not wholesome, because it is too unequal. The feeling in Natal is too bitter. The feeling in the Cape is too contemptuous. There is no more reason for one sentiment than for the other, and both are, in the best interests of South Africa, to be regretted. Natal and the Cape Colony ought to work hand in hand. They would soon find, if they could agree to do so, that they have both everything to gain ; for the development of the interior, which they would agree to further, is as much to the advantage of the one as of the other. The hindrance to this agreement lies, so far as a stranger is able to see, much more in the weakness of Natal than in the strength—even though that strength be sometimes overbearing—of the Cape. No doubt the bigger colony is inclined to be imperious, and to put the wishes and interests of its own electorate before every other consideration. This is only to be expected, in view of human imperfection. But, if Natal could rid itself of over-sensitiveness in the matter, and consider the questions with which the two colonies are mutually concerned fairly and practically upon their own basis, it would probably find that it has much more to gain by accepting a reasonable compromise than by standing aloof in its present attitude of rigid opposition.

If the change from representative to responsible government were to have no other effect than that of softening the asperity of local sentiment, and inspiring the leaders of public opinion in Natal with an easier sense of the dignity and security of their own position, it would, for this reason alone, be worth an effort to secure. Practical objections may prove overwhelming. On general grounds everything which tends to raise the position of Natal, and to place her on terms of equality with the other Governments of South Africa, is in itself desirable.

It is impossible to travel through this lovely and fertile corner of the Continent without recognising in it an epitome of the two main interests of South Africa. Material development and the race question are here laid out, as it were, visibly side by side, so close one to the other that each throws the other into relief. The train journey from Durban to Maritzburg, lying all the way through fruit gardens and farms, and rising so steeply that without putting your head out of the window you see the engine constantly on the opposite sweep of a curve before you, presents a typical picture of what European energy can achieve.

On the coast the town of Durban is one of which any small population might be justly proud. But, as you mount in the course of the same train journey to the higher levels and obtain a magnificent and commanding view of the surrounding country, you realise that the towns and the train and the richly cultivated land on either side form only a strip of civilised development which is drawn like a riband across an area of native wildness. Kaffirs swarm visibly on every side, and their presence forces on your comprehension the fact that they occupy the country in an immense numerical majority to the white population. The features of the position are slightly accentuated here, but this is in fact the position of South Africa as a whole. Like Natal, it is crossed by lines and currents of civilisation. Like Natal, it possesses still wide areas untouched by development. Like Natal, its native population greatly outnumbers the governing body of Europeans. The problems of the parts are the problems of the whole, and there is so complete an identity of interests that there is everything to gain from co-operation. Co-operation, in fact, is the master word of South African politics.

Printed by R. & R. CLARK, *Edinburgh.*

www.ingramcontent.com/pod-product-compliance
Lightning Source LLC
Chambersburg PA
CBHW020128170426
43199CB00009B/682